THE MIGRATIONS
OF EARLY CULTURE

LECTOR HOUSE PUBLIC DOMAIN WORKS

THE MIGRATIONS OF EARLY CULTURE

GRAFTON ELLIOT SMITH

ISBN: 978-93-5614-353-1

Published: 1915

LECTOR HOUSE LLP
E-MAIL: lectorpublishing@gmail.com

UNIVERSITY OF MANCHESTER PUBLICATIONS
NO. CII.

THE MIGRATIONS OF EARLY CULTURE

A STUDY OF THE SIGNIFICANCE OF THE GEOGRAPHICAL DISTRIBUTION OF THE PRACTICE OF MUMMIFICATION AS EVIDENCE OF THE MIGRATIONS OF PEOPLES AND THE SPREAD OF CERTAIN CUSTOMS AND BELIEFS

BY

GRAFTON ELLIOT SMITH, M.A., M.D., F.R.S.,

Professor of Anatomy in the University

1915

PREFACE.

When these pages were crudely flung together no fate was contemplated for them other than that of publication in the proceedings of a scientific society, as an appeal to ethnologists to recognise the error of their ways and repent. They were intended merely as a mass of evidence to force scientific men to recognise and admit that in former ages knowledge and culture spread in much the same way as they are known to be diffused to-day. The only difference is that the pace of migration has become accelerated.

The re-publication in book form was suggested by the Secretary of the Manchester University Press, who thought that the matters discussed in these pages would appeal to a much wider circle of readers than those who are given to reading scientific journals.

The argument is compounded largely of extracts from the writings of recognised authorities, and the author does not agree with all the statements in the various extracts he has quoted: this mode of presenting the case has been adopted deliberately, with the object of demonstrating that the generally admitted facts are capable of a more natural and convincing explanation than that put forth *ex cathedra* by the majority of modern anthropologists, one in fact more in accord with all that our own experience and the facts of history teach us of the effects of the contact of peoples and the spread of knowledge.

Such a method of stating the argument necessarily involves a considerable amount of repetition of statements and phrases, which is apt to irritate the reader and offend his sense of literary style. In extenuation of this admitted defect it must be remembered that the brochure was intended as a protest against the accusation of artificiality and improbability so often launched against the explanation suggested here: the cumulative effect of corroboration was deliberately aimed at, by showing that many investigators employing the most varied kinds of data had independently arrived at identical conclusions and often expressed them in similar phrases.

Only a very small fraction of the evidence is set forth in the present work. Much of the most illuminating information has only come to the author's knowledge since this memoir was in the press; and a vast amount of the data, especially that relating to Europe, India and China, is too intimately intertwined with the effects of other cultures to be discussed and dissociated from them in so limited a space as this.

Nor has any attempt been made to discuss the times of the journeys, the duration of the intercourse, or the details of the goings and the comings of the ancient mariners who distributed so curious an assortment of varied cargoes to the coast-lines of the whole world—literally "from China to Peru." They exerted an influence upon the history of civilization and achieved marvels of maritime daring that must be reckoned of greater account, as they were so many ages earlier, than those of the more notorious mediæval European adventurers and buccaneers who, impelled by similar motives, raided the Spanish Main and the East Indies.

As the pages show, this book is reprinted from volume 59, part 2, of the "Memoirs and Proceedings of the Manchester Literary and Philosophical Society," session 1914-15; and I am indebted to the Council of that body for their kind permission to re-issue it in its present form.

G. Elliot Smith.

The University,
Manchester,
July, 1915.

CONTENTS

LIST OF ILLUSTRATIONS

MANCHESTER MEMOIRS,
VOL. LIX. (1915), NO. 10.

X. ON THE SIGNIFICANCE OF THE GEOGRAPHICAL DISTRIBUTION OF THE PRACTICE OF MUMMIFICATION.—A STUDY OF THE MIGRATIONS OF PEOPLES AND THE SPREAD OF CERTAIN CUSTOMS AND BELIEFS.

BY PROFESSOR G. ELLIOT SMITH, M.A., M.D., F.R.S.

(*Read February 23rd, 1915. Received for publication April 6th, 1915.*)

In entering upon the discussion of the geographical distribution of the practice of mummification I am concerned not so much with the origin and technical procedures of this remarkable custom. This aspect of the problem I have already considered in a series of memoirs (**75 to 89**[1]). I have chosen mummification rather as the most peculiar, and therefore the most distinctive and obtrusive, element of a very intimately interwoven series of strange customs, which became fortuitously linked one with the other to form a definite culture-complex nearly thirty centuries ago, and spread along the coast-lines of a great part of the world, stirring into new and distinctive activity the sluggish uncultured peoples which in turn were subjected to this exotic leaven.

If one looks into the journals of anthropology and ethnology, there will be found amongst the vast collections of information relating to man's activities a most suggestive series of facts concerning the migrations of past ages and the spread of peculiar customs and beliefs.

---

[1] These figures refer to the bibliography at the end.

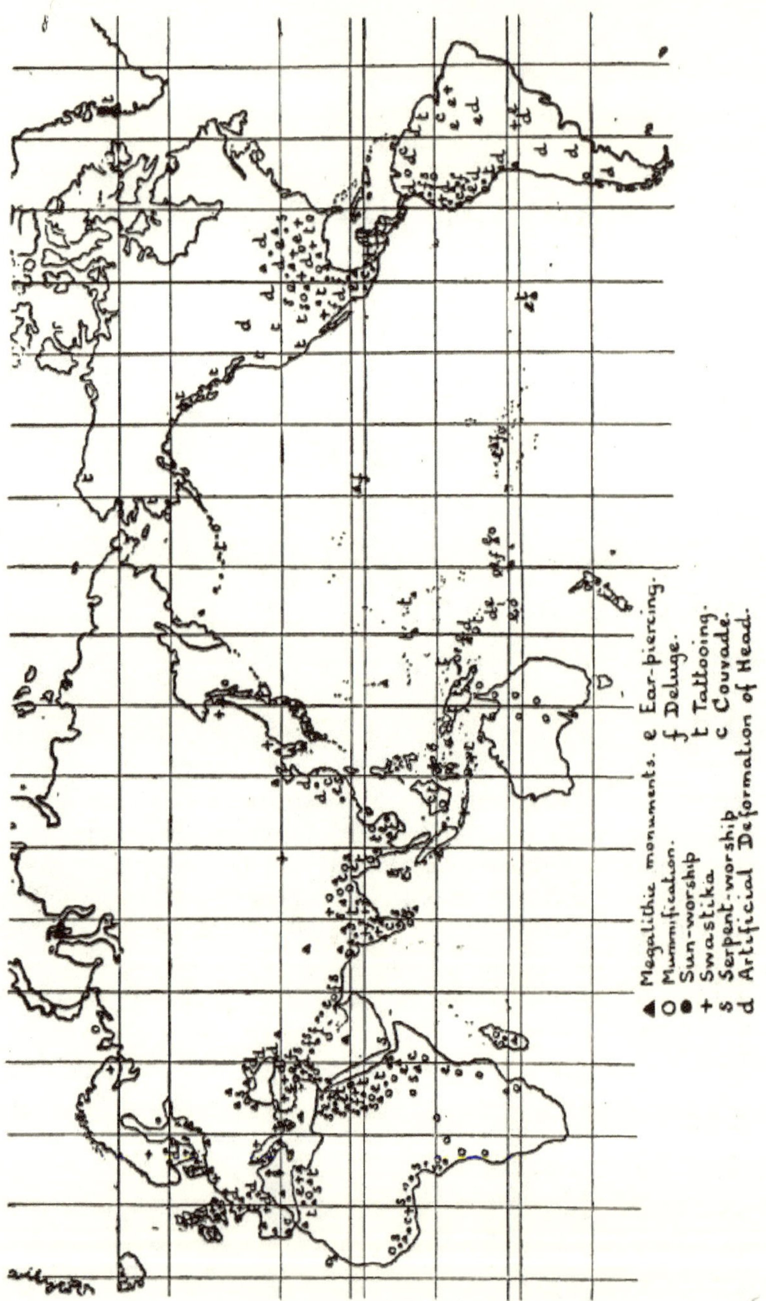

Map 1.—A rough chart of the geographical distribution of certain customs, practices and traditions. [None of these areas of distribution is complete. The map shows merely the data referred to in this memoir or in the literature quoted in it.]

If a map of the world is taken and one plots out (*Map I.*) the geographical distribution of such remarkable customs as the building of megalithic monuments (see for example Lane Fox's [Pitt Rivers'] map, **20**), the worship of the sun and the serpent (**51; 103**), the custom of piercing the ears (see Park Harrison, **29**), tattooing (see Miss Buckland, **10**), the practice of circumcision, the curious custom known as couvade, the practice of massage, the complex story of the creation, the deluge, the petrifaction of human beings, the divine origin of kings and a chosen people sprung from an incestuous union (W. J. Perry), the use of the swastika-symbol (see Wilson's map, **105**), the practice of cranial deformation, to mention only a few of the many that might be enumerated, it will be found that in most respects the areas in which this extraordinary assortment of bizarre customs and beliefs is found coincide one with the other. In some of the series gaps occur, which probably are more often due to lack of information on our part than to real absence of the practice; in other places one or other of the elements of this complex culture-mixture has overflowed the common channel and broken into new territory. But considered in conjunction these data enable us definitely and precisely to map out the route taken by this peculiarly distinctive group of eccentricities of the human mind. If each of them is considered alone there are many breaks in the chain and many uncertainties as to the precise course: but when taken together all of these gaps are bridged. Moreover, in most areas there are traditions of culture-heroes, who brought in some or all of these customs at one and the same time and also introduced a knowledge of agriculture and weaving.

So far as I am aware no one hitherto has called attention to the fact that the practice of mummification has a geographical distribution exactly corresponding to the area occupied by the curious assortment of other practices just enumerated. Not only so, but in addition it is abundantly clear that the coincidence is not merely accidental. It is due to the fact that in most regions the people who introduced the habit of megalithic building and sun-worship (a combination for which it is convenient to use Professor Brockwell's distinctive term "heliolithic culture") also brought with them the practice of mummification at the same time.

The custom of embalming the dead is in fact an integral part of the "heliolithic culture," and perhaps, as I shall endeavour to demonstrate, its most important component. For this practice and the beliefs which grew up in association with it were responsible for the development of some of the chief elements of this culture-complex, and incidentally of the bond of union with other factors not so intimately connected, in the genetic sense, with it.

Before plunging into the discussion of the evidence provided by the practice of mummification, it will be useful to consider for a moment the geographical distribution of the other components of the "heliolithic culture." I need not say much about megalithic monuments, for I have already considered their significance elsewhere (**90 to 96**); but I should like once more specifically to call the attention of those who are obsessed by theories of the independent evolution of such monuments, and who scoff at Fergusson (**17**), to the memoirs of Lane Fox (**20**) and Meadows Taylor (**100**). The latter emphasises in a striking manner the remarkable identity of structure, not only as concerns the variety and the general conception of such monuments, but also as regards trivial and apparently unessential details. With reference to "the opinion of many," which has "been advanced as an hypothesis, that the common instincts of humanity have suggested common methods of sepulture," he justly remarks, "I own this kind of vague generalisation does not satisfy me, in the face of such exact points of similitude.... Such can hardly have been the result of accident, or any common human instinct" (p. 173).

But it is not merely the identity of structure and the geographical distribution (in most cases along continuous coast-lines or related islands) that proves the common origin of megalithic monuments. It is further strongly corroborated by a remarkable series of beliefs, traditions and practices, many of them quite meaningless and unintelligible to us, which are associated with such structures wherever they are found. Stories of dwarfs and giants (**13**), the belief in the indwelling of gods or great men in the stones, the use of these structures in a particular manner for certain special councils (**20**, pp. 64 and 65), and the curious, and, to us, meaningless, practice of hanging rags on trees in association with such monuments (**20**, pp. 63 and 64). In reference to the last of these associated practices, Lane Fox remarks, "it is impossible to believe that so singular a custom as this could have arisen independently in all these countries."

In an important article on "Facts suggestive of prehistoric intercourse between East and West" (*Journ. Anthr. Inst.*, Vol. 14, 1884, p. 227), Miss Buckland calls attention to a remarkable series of identities of customs and beliefs, and amongst them certain legends concerning the petrification of *dance maidens* associated with stone circles as far apart as Cornwall and Peru.

Taking all of these facts into consideration, it is to me altogether inconceivable how any serious enquirer who familiarises himself with the evidence can honestly refuse to admit that the case for the spread of the inspiration to erect megalithic monuments from one centre has been proved by an overwhelming mass of precise and irrefutable data. But this evidence does not stand alone. It is linked with scores of other peculiar customs and beliefs, the testimony of each of which, however imperfect and unconvincing some scholars may consider it individually, strengthens the whole case by cumulation; and when due consideration is given to the enormous complexity and artificiality of the cultural structure compounded of such fantastic elements, these are bound to compel assent to their significance, as soon as the present generation of ethnologists can learn to forget the meaningless fetish to which at present it bends the knee.

But suppose, for the sake of argument, we shut our ears to the voice of common sense, and allow ourselves to be hypnotised into the belief that some complex and highly specialised instinct (*i.e.* precisely the type of instinct which real psychologists—not the ethnological variety—deny to mankind) impelled groups of men scattered as far apart as Ireland, India and Peru independently the one of the other to build mausolea of the same type, to acquire similar beliefs regarding the petrifaction of human beings, and many other extraordinary things connected with such monuments, how is this "psychological explanation" going to help us to explain why the wives of the builders of these monuments, whether in Africa, Asia or America, should have their chins pricked and rubbed with charcoal, or why they should circumcise their boys, or why they should have a tradition of the deluge? Does any theory of evolution help in explaining these associations? They are clearly fortuitous associations of customs and beliefs, which have no inherent relationship one to the other. They became connected purely by chance in one definite locality, and the fact that such incongruous customs reappear in association in distant parts of the globe is proof of the most positive kind that the wanderings of peoples must have brought this peculiar combination of freakish practices from the centre where chance linked them together.

Because it was the fashion among a particular group of megalith-builders to tattoo the chins of their womenkind, the wanderers who carried abroad the one custom also took the other: but there is no genetic or inherent connection between megalith-building and chin-tattooing.

Such evidence is infinitely stronger and more convincing than that afforded by one custom considered by itself, because in the former case we are dealing with an association which is definitely and obviously due to pure chance, such as the so-called psychological method, however casuistical, is impotent to explain.

But the study of such a custom as tattooing, even when considered alone, affords evidence that ought to convince most reasonable people of the impossibility of it having independently arisen in different, widely scattered, localities. The data have been carefully collected and discussed with clear insight and common sense by Miss Buckland (**10**) in an admirable memoir, which I should like to commend to all who still hold to the meaningless dogma "of the similarity of the working of the human mind" as an explanation of the identity of customs. Tattooing is practised throughout the great "heliolithic" track. [Striking as Miss Buckland's map of distribution is as a demonstration of this, if completed in the light of our present information, it would be even more convincing, for she has omitted Libya, which so far as we know at present may possibly have been the centre of origin of the curious practice.]

Tattooing of the chin in women is practised in localities as far apart as Egypt, India, Japan, New Guinea, New Zealand, Easter Island and North and South America.

Miss Buckland rightly draws the conclusion that "the wide distribution of this peculiar custom is of considerable significance, especially as it follows so nearly in the line" which she had "indicated in two previous papers (**8** and **9**) as suggestive of a prehistoric intercourse between the two hemispheres.... When we find in India, Japan, Egypt, New Guinea, New Zealand, Alaska, Greenland and America, the custom of tattooing carried out in precisely the same manner and for the same ends, and when in addition to this we find a similarity in other ornaments, in weapons, in games, in modes of burial, and many other customs, we think it may fairly be assumed that they all derived these customs from a common source, or that at some unknown period, some intercourse existed" (p. 326).

In the first of her memoirs (**8**) Miss Buckland calls attention to "the curious connection between early worship of the serpent and a knowledge of metals," which is of peculiar interest in this discussion, because the Proto-Egyptians, who were serpent-worshippers (*see* Sethe, **74**), had a knowledge of metals at a period when, so far as our present knowledge goes, no other people had yet acquired it. Referring to the ancient Indian Indra, the Chaldean Ea and the Mexican Quetzalcoatl, among other gods, Miss Buckland remarks:—"The deities, kings and heroes who are symbolised by the serpent are commonly described as the pioneers of civilisation and the instructors of mankind in the arts of agriculture and mining."

Further, in an interesting article on "Stimulants in Use among Savages and among the Ancients" (**9**), she tells us that "among aboriginal races in a line across the Pacific, from Formosa on the West to Peru and Bolivia on the East, a peculiar, and what would appear to civilised races a disgusting mode of preparing fermented drinks, prevails, the women being in all cases the chief manufacturers; the material employed varying according to the state of agriculture in the different localities, but the mode of preparation remaining virtually the same" (**9**, p. 213).

If space permitted I should have liked to make extensive quotations from Park Harrison's most conclusive independent demonstration of the spread of culture along the same great route, at which he arrived from the study of the geographical distribution of the peculiar custom of artificially distending the lobe of the ear (**29**). This practice was not infrequent in Egypt (**79**) in the times of the new Empire, a fact which Harrison seems to have overlooked: but he records it amongst the Greeks, Hebrews, Etruscans, Persians, in Bœotia, Zanzibar, Natal, Southern India, Ceylon, Assam, Aracan, Burma, Laos, Nicobar Islands, Nias, Borneo, China, Solomon Islands, Admiralty Islands, New Hebrides, New Caledonia, Pelew Islands, Navigators Island, Fiji, Friendly Islands, Penrhyn, Society Islands, Easter Island, Peru, Palenque, Mexico, Brazil and Paraguay. This is an excellent and remarkably complete [if he had used the data now available it might have been made even more complete] mapping out of the great "heliolithic" track.

The identity of geographical distribution is no mere fortuitous coincidence.

It is of peculiar interest that Harrison is able to demonstrate a linked association between this custom and sun-worship in most of the localities enumerated. In the figures illustrating his memoir other obvious associations can be detected intimately binding it by manifold threads into the very texture of the "heliolithic culture." If to this we add the fact that in many localities the design tattooed on the skin was the sun, we further strengthen the woof of the closely woven fabric that is gradually taking shape.

To these forty-year-old demonstrations let me add Wilson's interesting recent monograph on the swastika (**105**), which independently tells the same story and blazens the same great track around the world (see his map). He further calls attention to the close geographical association between the distribution of the swastika and the spindle-whorl. By attributing the introduction of weaving and the swastika into most localities where they occur by the same culture-heroes he thereby adds the swastika to the "heliolithic" outfit, for weaving already belongs to it.

To these practices one might add a large series of others of a character no less remarkable, such, for example, as circumcision, the practice of massage (**57**, **67** and **11**), the curious custom known as *couvade*, all of which are distributed along the great "heliolithic" pathway and belong to the great culture-complex which travelled by it.

But there are several interesting bits of corroborative evidence that I cannot refrain from mentioning.

One of the most carefully-investigated bonds of cultural connection between the Eastern Mediterranean in Phœnician times and pre-Columbian America (Tehuantepec) has recently been put on record by Zelia Nuttall in her memoir on "a curious survival in Mexico of the use of the Purpura shell-fish for dyeing" (**50**). After a very thorough and critical analysis of all the facts of this truly remarkable case of transmission of an extraordinary custom, Mrs. Nuttall justly concludes that "it seems almost easier to believe that certain elements of an ancient European culture were at one time, and perhaps once only, actually transmitted by the traditional small band of ... Mediterranean seafarers, than to explain how, under totally different conditions of race and climate, the identical ideas and customs should have arisen" (pp. 383 and 384). Nor does she leave us in any doubt as to the route taken by the carriers of this practice. Found in association with it, both in the Old and the New World, was the use of conch-shell trumpets and pearls. The antiquity of these usages is proved by their representation in pre-Columbian pictures or, in the case of the pearls, the finding of actual specimens in graves.

In Phœnician Greek, and later times these shell-trumpets were extensively used in the Mediterranean: "European travellers have found them in actual use in East India, Japan and, by the Alfurs, in Ceram, the Papuans of New Guinea, as well as in the South Sea islands as far as New Zealand," and in many places in America (p. 378). "In the Old and the New World alike, are found, in the same close association, (1) the purple industry and skill in weaving; (2) the use of pearls and conch-shell trumpets; (3) the mining, working and trafficking in copper, silver and gold; (4) the tetrarchial form of government; (5) the conception of 'Four Elements'; (6) the cyclical form of calendar. Those scholars who assert that all of the foregoing must have been developed independently will ever be confronted by the persistent and unassailable fact that, throughout America, the aborigines unanimously disclaim all share in their production and assign their introduction to strangers of superior-culture from distant and unknown parts" (p. 383).

Many other equally definite proofs might be cited of the transmission of customs from the Old to the New World, of which the instance reported by Tylor (**102**) is the classical example[2]; but I know of no other which has been so critically studied and so fully recorded as Mrs. Nuttall's case.

---

[2] Tylor ("On the Game of Patolli," *Journ. Anthrop. Inst.*, Vol. VIII., 1879, p. 128) cites another certain case of borrowing on the part of pre-Columbian America from Asia. "Lot-backgammon as represented by tab, *pachisi*, etc., ranges in the Old World from Egypt across Southern Asia to Birma. As the *patolli* of the Mexicans is a variety of lot-backgammon most nearly approaching the Hindu *pachisi*, and perhaps like it passing into the stage of dice-backgammon, its presence seems to prove that it had made its way across from Asia. At any rate, it may be reckoned among elements of Asiatic culture traceable in the old Mexican civilization, the high development of which ... seems to be in large measure due to Asiatic influence."

But the difficulty may be raised—as in fact invariably happens when these subjects come up for discussion—as to the means of transmission. Rivers has explained what does actually happen in the contact of peoples (**68**) and how a small group of wanderers bringing the elements of a higher culture can exert a profound and far-reaching influence upon a large uncultured population (**64** to **70**).

Lane-Fox's [Pitt Rivers'] memoir "on Early Modes of Navigation" (**21**) not only affords in itself an admirable summary of the definite evidence for the spread of culture; but is also doubly valuable to us, because incidentally it illustrates also the actual means by which the migrations of the culture-bearers took place. The survival into modern times, upon the Hooghly and other Indian rivers, of boats provided with the fantastic steering arrangement used by the Ancient Egyptians 2000 years B.C., is in itself a proof of ancient Egyptian influence in India; and the contemporary practice of representing eyes upon the bow of the ship enables us to demonstrate a still wider extension of that influence, for in modern times that custom has been recorded as far apart as Malta, India, China, Oceania and the North-West American coast.

But there is no difficulty about the question of the transmission of such customs. Most scholars who have mastered the early history of some particular area, in many cases those who most resolutely deny even the possibility of the wider spread of culture, frankly admit—because it would stultify their own localised researches to deny it—the intercourse of the particular people in which they are interested and its neighbours. Merely by using these links, forged by the reluctant hands of hostile witnesses, it is possible to construct the whole chain needed for such migrations as I postulate (see *Map II.*)

No one who reads the evidence collected by such writers as Ellis (**15**), de Quatrefages (**60**) and Percy Smith (**98**)[3] can doubt the fact of the extensive prehistoric migrations throughout the Pacific Ocean along definitely known routes. Even Joyce (whose otherwise excellent summaries of the facts relating to American archæology have been emasculated by his refusal to admit the influence of the Old World upon American culture) states that migrations from India extended to Indonesia (and Madagascar) and all the islands of the Pacific; and even that "it is likely that the coast of America was reached" (**61**, p. 119).[4]

There is no doubt as to the reality of the close maritime intercourse between the Persian Gulf and India from the eighth century B.C. (**13**; **14**; **51**; and **101**); and of course it is a historical fact that the Mediterranean littoral and Egypt had been in intimate connexion with Babylonia for some centuries before, and especially after, that time.

---

[3] See also **2**; **3**; **7**; **8**; **9**; **10**; **16**; **20**; **21**; **24**; **29**; **30**; **38**; **48**; **49**; **50**; **51**; **61**; **73**; **103**; and **105**.
[4] For proof that it was reached see **3**; **8**; **9**; **10**; **20**; **21**; **38**; **49**; **50**; **51**; **73**; **102**; **103**; and **105**.

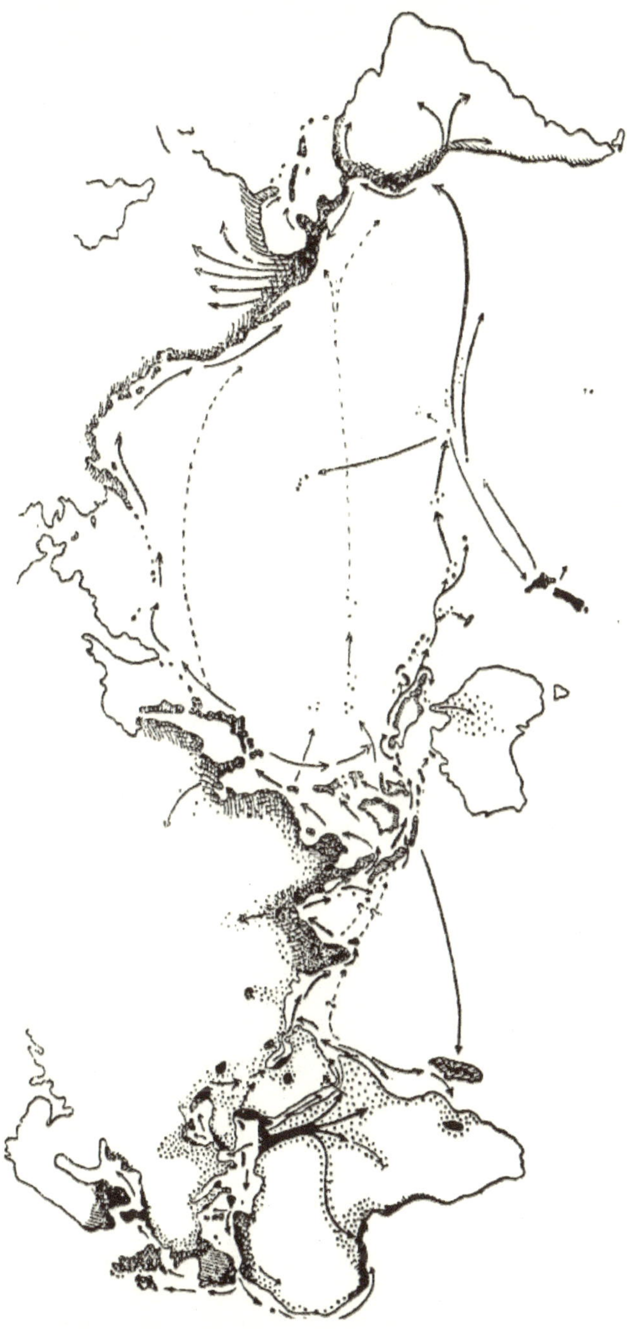

Map 2.— An attempt to represent roughly the areas more directly affected by the "heliolithic" culture-complex, with arrows to indicate the hypothetical routes taken in the migrations of the culture-bearers who were responsible for its diffusion.

In the face of this overwhelming mass of definite evidence of the reality not only of the spread of culture and its carriers, but also of the ways and the means by which it travelled, it will naturally be asked how it has come to pass that there is even the shadow of a doubt as to the migrations which distributed this "heliolithic" culture-complex so widely in the world. It cannot be explained by lack of knowledge, for most of the facts that I have enumerated are taken bodily from the anthropological journals of forty or more years ago.

The explanation is to be found, I believe, in a curious psychological process incidental to the intensive study of an intricate problem. As knowledge increased and various scholars attempted to define the means by (and the time at) which the contacts of various peoples took place, difficulties were revealed which, though really trivial, were magnified into insuperable obstacles. All of these real difficulties were created by mistaken ideas of the relative chronology of the appearance of civilisation in various centres, and especially by the failure to realise that useful arts were often lost. For example, if on a certain mainland A two practices, a and b—one of them, a, a useful practice, say the making of pottery; the other, b, a useless custom, say the preservation of the corpse—were developed, and a was at least as old, or preferably definitely older than b, it seemed altogether inconceivable to the ethnologist if an island B was influenced by the culture of the mainland A, at some time after the practices a and b were in vogue, that it might, under any conceivable circumstances, fail to preserve the useful art a, even though it might allow the utterly useless practice b to lapse. Therefore it was argued that, if the later inhabitants of B mummified their dead, but did not make pottery, this was clear evidence that they could not have come under the influence of A.

But the whole of the formidable series of obstacles raised by this kind of argument has been entirely swept away by Dr. Rivers, who has demonstrated how often it has happened that a population has completely lost some useful art which it once had, and even more often clung to some useless practice (**65**).

The remarkable feature of the present state of the discussion is that, in spite of Rivers' complete demolition of these difficulties (**65**), most ethnologists do not seem to realise that there is now a free scope for taking a clear and common-sense view of the truth, unhindered by any obstructions. It is characteristic of the history of scientific, no less than of theological argument, that the immediate effect of the destruction of the foundations of cherished beliefs is to make their more fanatical votaries shout their creed all the louder and more dogmatically, and hurl anathemas at those who dissent.

This is the only explanation I can offer of the remarkable presidential address delivered by Fewkes to the Anthropological Society of Washington in 1912 (**18**), Keane's incoherent recklessness[5] (**41**, pp. 140, 218, 219, and 367 to 370), and the

---

[5] Dr. Fewkes' discourse is essentially a farrago of meaningless verbiage. Later on in this communication I shall give a characteristic sample of the late Professor Keane's dialectic; but the whole of the passages referred to should be read by anyone who is inclined to cavil at my strictures upon such expositions of modern ethnological doctrine. The obvious course for any serious investigator to pursue is to ignore such superficial and illogical pretensions: but the ethnological literature of this country and America is so permeated with

amazing criticisms which during the last four years I have had annually to meet. There is no attempt at argument, but mere dogmatic and often irrelevant assertions. The constant appeal to the meaningless phrase "the similarity of the working of the human mind"[6] (**18**), as though it were a magical incantation against logical induction, and harping on the so-called "psychological argument" (**41**), which is directly opposed to the teaching of psychology, are the only excuses one can obtain from the "orthodox" ethnologist for this obstinate refusal to face the issue. Of course it is a historical fact that the discussions of the theory of evolution inclined ethnologists during the last century the more readily to accept the *laisser faire* attitude, and put an end to all their difficulties by the pretence that most cultures developed independently *in situ*. It is all the more surprising that Huxley took some small part in encouraging this lapse into superficiality and abuse of the evolution conception, when it is recalled that, as Sir Michael Foster tells us, the then President of the Ethnological Society "made himself felt in many ways, not the least by the severity with which he repressed the pretensions of shallow persons who, taking advantage of the glamour of the Darwinian doctrine, talked nonsense in the name of anthropological science" ("Life and Letters of Thomas Henry Huxley," Vol. I., p. 263).

It is a singular commentary on the attitude of the "orthodox" school of ethnologists that, when pressed to accept the obvious teaching of ethnological evidence, they should desert the strong intrenchments which the difficulties of full and adequate explanation have afforded them in the past, and take refuge behind the straw barricades of imaginary psychological and biological analogies, which they have hastily constructed for their own purposes, and in flagrant defiance of all that the psychologist understands by the phrase "working of the human mind," if perchance he is ever driven to employ this expression, or the meaning attached by the biologist to "evolution."

It is not sufficient proof of my thesis, however, merely to expose the hollowness of the pretensions of one's opponents, nor even to show the identity of geographical distribution and the linking up of customs to form the "heliolithic" culture-complex. Many writers have dimly realised that some such spread of culture took place, but by misunderstanding the nature of the factors that came into play or the chronology of the movements they were discussing (see especially Macmil-

---

ideas such as Fewkes and Keane express, that it has become necessary bluntly to expose the utter hollowness of their case.

[6] For if any sense whatever is to be attached to this phrase it implies that man is endowed with instincts of a much more complex and highly specialised kind than any insect or bird—instincts moreover which impel a group of men to perform at the same epoch a very large series of peculiarly complex, meaningless and fantastic acts that have no possible relationship to the "struggle for existence," which is supposed to be responsible for the fashioning of instincts.

But William McDougall tells us that the distinctive feature of human instincts is that they are of "the most highly general type." "They merely provide a basis for vaguely directed activities in response to vaguely discriminated impressions from large classes of objects." ("Psychology, the Study of Behaviour," p. 171.) There is nothing vague about the extraordinary repertoire of the "heliolithic" cult!

lan Brown's (**7**) and Enoch's (**16**) books, to mention the latest, but by no means the worst offenders), have brought discredit upon the thesis I am endeavouring to demonstrate.

Another danger has arisen out of the revulsion against Bastian's old idea of independent evolution by his fellow-countrymen Frobenius, Graebner, Ankermann, Foy and others, with the co-operation of the Austrian philologist, Schmidt, and the Swiss ethnologist, Montandon (who has summarised the views of the new school in the first part of the new journal, *Archives suisses d'Anthropologie générale*, May, 1914, p. 113); for they have rushed to the other extreme, and, relying mainly upon objects of "material culture," have put forward a method of analysis and postulated a series of migrations for which the evidence is very doubtful. Rivers (**64**) has pointed out the unreliability of such inferences when unchecked by the consideration of elements of culture which are not so easily bartered or borrowed as bows and spears. He has insisted upon the fundamental importance of the study of social organisation as supplying the most stable and trustworthy data for the analysis of a culture-complex and an index of racial admixture. The study of such a practice as mummification, the influence of which is deep-rooted in the innermost beliefs of the people who resort to it, affords data almost as reliable as Rivers' method; for the subsequent account will make it abundantly clear that the practice of embalming leaves its impress upon the burial customs of a people long ages after other methods of disposal of their dead have been adopted.

I have been led into this digression by attempting to make it clear that the mere demonstration of the identity of geographical distribution and the linking together of a series of cultural elements by no means represents the solution of the main problem.

What has still to be elucidated is the manner and the place in which the complex fabric of the "heliolithic" culture was woven, the precise epoch in which it began to be spread abroad and the identity of its carriers, the influences to which it was subjected on the way, and the additions, subtractions and modifications which it underwent as the result.

Although I have now collected many of the data for the elucidation of these points, the limited space at my disposal compels me to defer for the present the consideration of the most interesting aspect of the whole problem, the identity of the early mariners who were the distributors of so strange a cargo. It was this aspect of the question which first led me into the controversy; but I shall be able to deal with it more conveniently when the ethnological case has been stated. The enormous bulk of the data that have accumulated compels me to omit a large mass of corroborative evidence of an ethnological nature; but no doubt there will be many opportunities in the near future for using up this reserve of ammunition.

Before setting out for the meeting of the British Association in Australia last year I submitted the following abstract of a communication (**96**) to be made to the Section of Anthropology:—

"After dealing with the evidence from the resemblances in the physical characteristics of widely separated populations—such, for instance, as certain of the ancient inhabitants of Western Asia on the one hand, and certain Polynesians on the other—suggesting far-reaching prehistoric migrations, the distribution of certain peculiarly distinctive practices, such as mummification and the building of megalithic monuments, is made use of to confirm the reality of such wanderings of peoples.

"I have already (at the Portsmouth, Dundee, and Birmingham meetings) dealt with the problem as it affects the Mediterranean littoral and Western Europe. On the present occasion I propose to direct attention mainly to the question of the spread of culture from the centres of the ancient civilisations along the Southern Asiatic coast and from there out into the Pacific. From the examination of the evidence supplied by megalithic monuments and distinctive burial customs, studied in the light of the historical information relating to the influence exerted by Arabia and India in the Far East, one can argue by analogy as to the nature of migrations in the even more remote past to explain the distribution of the earliest peoples dwelling on the shores of the Pacific.

"Practices such as mummification and megalith-building present so many peculiar and distinctive features that no hypothesis of independent evolution can seriously be entertained in explanation of their geographical distribution. They must be regarded as evidence of the diffusion of information, and the migrations of bearers of it, from somewhere in the neighbourhood of the Eastern Mediterranean, step by step out into Polynesia, and even perhaps beyond the Pacific to the American littoral."

At that time it was my intention further to develop the arguments from megalithic monuments which I had laid before the Association at the three preceding meetings and elsewhere (**90**; **91**; **92**; **93**; and especially **94**); and endeavour to prove that the structure and the geographical distribution of these curious memorials pointed to the spread of a distinctive type of culture along the Southern Asiatic littoral, through Indonesia and Oceania to the American Continent. The geographical distribution of the practice of mummification was to have been used merely as a means of corroboration of what I then imagined to be the more complete megalithic record, and of emphasizing the fact that Egypt had played some part at least in originating these curiously linked customs.

But when I examined the mummy from Torres Straits in the Macleay Museum (University of Sydney), and studied the literature relating to the methods employed by the embalmers in that region (**1**; **19**; **25**; and **27**), I was convinced, from my knowledge of the technical details used in mummification in ancient Egypt (see especially **78**; **86** and **87**), that these Papuan mummies supplied us with the most positive demonstration of the Egyptian origin of the methods employed. Moreover, as they revealed a series of very curious procedures, such as were not invented in Egypt until the time of the New Empire, and some of them not until the XXIst Dynasty, it was evident that the cultural wave which carried the knowledge of these things to the Torres Straits could not have started on its long course from Egypt before the ninth century B.C., at the earliest.

The incision for eviscerating the body was made in the flank, right or left, or in the perineum (**19**; **25**)—the two sites selected for making the embalming incision in Egypt (**78**); the flank incision was made in the precise situation (between costal margin and iliac crest) which was distinctive of XXIst and XXIInd Dynasty methods in Egypt (**86**); and the wound was stitched up in accordance with the method employed in the case of the cheaper kinds of embalming at that period (**78**). When the flank incision was not employed an opening was made in the perineum, as was done in Egypt—the second method mentioned by Herodotus—in the case of less wealthy people (**56**, p. 46).

The viscera, after removal, were thrown into the sea, as, according to Porphyry and Plutarch, it was the practice in Egypt at one time (**56**, pp. 57 and 58) to cast them into the Nile.

The body was painted with a mixture containing red-ochre, the scalp was painted black, and artificial eyes were inserted. These procedures were first adopted (in their entirety) in Egypt during the XXIst Dynasty, although the experiments leading up to the adoption of these methods began in the XIXth.

But most remarkable of all, the curiously inexplicable Egyptian procedure for removing the brain, which in Egypt was not attempted until the XVIIIth Dynasty—*i.e.*, until its embalmers had had seventeen centuries experience of their remarkable craft (**78**)—was also followed by the savages of the Torres Straits (**25**; **27**)!

Surely it is inconceivable that such people could have originated the idea or devised the means for practising an operation so devoid of meaning and so technically difficult as this! The interest of their technique is that the Torres Straits operators followed the method originally employed in Egypt (in the case of the mummy of the Pharaoh Ahmes I. [**86**, p. 16]), which is one requiring considerable skill and dexterity, and not the simpler operation through the nostrils which was devised later (**78**).

The Darnley Islanders also made a circular incision through the skin of each finger and toe, and having scraped off the epidermis from the rest of the body, they carefully peeled off these thimbles of skin, and presented them to the deceased's widow (**25**; **27**).

This practice is peculiarly interesting as an illustration of the adoption of an ancient Egyptian custom in complete ignorance of the purpose it was intended to serve. The ancient Egyptian embalmers (and, again, those of the XXIst Dynasty) made similar circular incisions around fingers and toes, and also scraped off the rest of the epidermis: but the aim of this strange procedure was to prevent the general epidermis, as it was shed (which occurred when the body was steeped for weeks in the preservative brine bath), from carrying the finger- and toe-nails with it (**78**). A thimble of skin was left on each finger and toe to keep the nail *in situ*; and to make it doubly secure, it was tied on with string (**78**) or fixed with a ring of gold or a silver glove (**84**).

In the Torres Straits method of embalming the brine bath was not used; so the scraping off of the epidermis was wholly unnecessary. In addition, after following precisely the preliminary steps of this aimless proceeding, by deliberately and intentionally removing the skin-thimbles and nails they defeated the very objects which the Egyptians had in view when they invented this operation!

An elaborate technical operation such as this which serves no useful purpose and is wholly misunderstood by its practitioners cannot have been invented by them. It is another certain proof of the Egyptian origin of the practice.

There is another feature of these Papuan mummies which may or may not be explicable as the adoption of Egyptian practices put to a modified, if not a wholly different, use. Among the new methods introduced in Egypt in the XXIst Dynasty was a curious device for restoring to the mummy something of the fulness of form and outline it had lost during the process of preservation. Through various incisions (which incidentally no doubt allowed the liquid products of decomposition to escape) foreign materials were packed under the skin of the mummy (**78; 87**). These incisions were made between the toes, sometimes at the knees, in the region of the shoulders, and sometimes in other situations (**78**). In the Papuan method of mummification "cuts were made on the knee-caps and between the fingers and toes; then holes were pierced in the cuts with an arrow so as to allow the liquids to drip from them" (Hamlyn-Harris, **27**, p. 3). In one of the mummies in the Brisbane museum there seem to be incisions also in the shoulders. The situation of these openings suggests the view that the idea of making them *may* (and I do not wish to put it any more definitely) have been suggested by the Egyptian XXIst Dynastic practice. For, although the incisions were made, in the latter case, for the purpose of packing the limbs, incidentally they served for drainage purposes.

But it was not only the mere method of embalming, convincing and definite as it is, that establishes the derivation of the Papuan from the Egyptian procedure; but also all the other funerary practices, and the beliefs associated with them, that help to clinch the proof. The special treatment of the head, the use of masks, the making of stone idols, these and scores of other curious customs (which have been described in detail in Haddon's and Myers' admirable account [**25**]) might be cited.

When I called the attention of the Anthropological Section to these facts and my interpretation of them at the meeting of the British Association in Melbourne, Professor J. L. Myres opened the discussion by adopting a line of argument which, even after four years' experience of controversies of the megalith-problem, utterly amazed me. "What more natural than that people should want to preserve their dead? Or that in doing so they should remove the more putrescible parts? Would not the flank be the natural place to choose for the purpose? Is it not a common practice for people to paint their dead with red-ochre?" It is difficult to believe that such questions were meant to be taken seriously. The claim that it is quite a natural thing on the death of a near relative for the survivors instinctively to remove his viscera, dry the corpse over a fire, scrape off his epidermis, remove his brain through a hole in the back of his neck, and then paint the corpse red is a sample of casuistry not unworthy of a mediæval theologian. Yet this is the gratuitous claim made at a scientific meeting! If Professor Myres had known anything of the history of Anatomy he would have realized that the problem of preserving the body was one of extreme difficulty which for long ages had exercised the most civilized peoples, not only in antiquity, but also in modern times. In Egypt, where the natural conditions favouring the successful issue of attempts to preserve the body were largely responsible for the possibility of such embalming, it took more than seventeen centuries of constant practice and experimentation to reach the stage and to acquire the methods exemplified in the Torres Straits mummies. In Egypt also a curious combination of natural circumstances and racial customs was responsible for the suggestion of the desirability and the possibility artificially to preserve the corpse. How did the people of the Torres Straits acquire the knowledge even of the possibility of such an attainment, not to mention the absence of any inherent suggestion of its desirability? For in the hot, damp atmosphere of such places as Darnley Island the corpse would never have been preserved by natural means, so that the suggestion which stimulated the Egyptians to embark upon their experimentation was lacking in the case of the Papuans. But even if for some mysterious reasons these people had been prompted to attempt to preserve their dead, during the experimental stage they would have had to combat these same unfavourable conditions. Is it at all probable or even possible to conceive that under such exceptionally difficult, not to say discouraging, circumstances they would have persisted for long periods in their gruesome experiments; or have attained a more rapid success than the more cultured peoples of Egypt and Europe, operating under more favourable climatic conditions, and with the help of a knowledge of chemistry and physics, were able to achieve? The suggestion is too preposterous to call for serious consideration.

But if for the moment we assume that the Darnley Islander instinctively arrived at the conclusion that it was possible to preserve the dead, that he would rather like to try it, and that by some mysterious inspiration the technical means of attaining this object was vouchsafed him, why, when the whole ventral surface of the body was temptingly inviting him to operate by the simplest and most direct means, did he restrict his choice to the two most difficult sites for his incision? We know why the Egyptian made the opening in the left flank and in other cases in the perineum; but is it likely the Papuan, once he had decided to cut the body, would have had such a respect for the preservation of the integrity of the front of the body as to impel him to choose a means of procedure which added greatly to the technical difficulty of the operation? We have the most positive evidence that the Papuan had no such design, for it was his usual procedure to cut the head off the trunk and pay little further attention to the latter. Myres' contention will not stand a moment's examination.

As to the use of red-ochre, which Myres rightly claimed to be so widespread, no hint was given of the possibility that it might be so extensively practised simply because the Egyptian custom had spread far and wide.

It is important to remember that the practice of painting stone statues with red-ochre (obviously to make them more life-like) was in vogue in Egypt before 3000 B.C.; and throughout the whole "heliolithic" area, wherever the conception of human beings dwelling in stones, whether carved or not, was adopted, the Egyptian practice of applying red paint also came into vogue. But it was not until more than twenty centuries later—*i.e.* when, for quite definite reasons in the XXIst Dynasty, the Egyptians conceived the idea of converting the mummy itself into a statue—that they introduced the procedure of painting the mummy (the actual body), simply because it was regarded as the statue (**78**).

After Professor Myres, Dr. Haddon offered two criticisms. Firstly, the incisions in the feet and knees were not suggested by Egyptian practices, but were made for the strictly utilitarian purpose of draining the fluids from the body. I have dealt with this point already (*vide supra*). His second objection was that there were no links between Egypt and Papua to indicate that the custom had spread. The present communication is intended to dispose of that objection by demonstrating not only the route by which, but also how, the practice reached the Torres Straits after the long journey from Egypt.

It will be noticed that this criticism leaves my main arguments from the mummies quite untouched. Moreover, the fact that originally I made use of the testimony of the mummies merely in support of evidence of other kinds (the physical characters of the peoples and the distribution of megalithic monuments) was completely ignored by my critics.

But, as I have already remarked, it is not merely the remarkable identity of so many of the peculiar features of Papuan and Egyptian embalming that affords definite evidence of the derivation of one from the other; but in addition, many of the ceremonies and practices, as well as the traditions relating to the people who introduced the custom of mummification, corroborate the fact that immigrants from the west introduced these elements of culture. In addition, they also suggest their affinities.

"A hero-cult, with masked performers and elaborate dances, spread from the mainland of New Guinea to the adjacent islands: part of this movement seems to have been associated with a funeral ritual that emphasised a life after death.... Most of the funeral ceremonies and many sacred songs admittedly came from the west" (Haddon, **25**, p. 45).

"Certain culture-heroes severally established themselves on certain islands, and they or their followers introduced a new cult which considerably modified the antecedent totemism," and taught "improved methods of cultivation and fishing" (p. 44).

"An interesting parallel to these hero-cults of Torres Straits occurred also in Fiji. The people of Viti-Levu trace their descent from [culture-heroes] who drifted across the Big Ocean and taught to the people the cult associated with the large stone enclosures" (p. 45).

In these islands the people were expert at carving stone idols and they had legends concerning certain "stones that once were men" (p. 11). It is also significant that at the bier of a near relative, boys and girls, who had arrived at the age of puberty, had their ears pierced and their skin tattooed (p. 154).

Thus Haddon himself supplies so many precise tokens of the "heliolithic" nature of the culture of the Torres Straits.

These hints of migrations and the coming of strangers bringing from the west curious practices and beliefs may seem at first sight to add little to the evidence afforded by the technique of the embalming process; but the subsequent discussion will make it plain that the association of these particular procedures with mummification serves to clinch the demonstration of the source from which that practice was derived.

It is doubly interesting to obtain all this corroborative evidence from the writings of Dr. Haddon, in view of the fact, to which I have already referred, that he vigorously protested against my contention that the embalmers of the Torres Straits acquired their art, directly or indirectly, from Egypt. For, in his graphic account of a burial ceremony at Murray Islands, his confession that, as he watched the funerary boat and the wailing women, his "mind wandered back thousands of years, and called up ancient Egypt carrying its dead in boats across the sacred Nile" has a much deeper and more real significance than he intended. The analogy which at once sprang to his mind was not merely a chance resemblance, but the expression of a definite survival amongst these simple people in the Far East of customs their remote ancestors had acquired, through many intermediaries no doubt, from the Egyptians of the ninth century B.C.

At the time when Dr. Haddon asked for the evidence for the connection between Egypt and Papua, I was aware only of the Burmese practices (*vide infra*) in the intervening area, and the problem of establishing the means by which the Egyptian custom actually spread seemed to be a very formidable task.

But soon after my return from Australia all the links in the cultural chain came to light. Mr. W. J. Perry, who had been engaged in analysing the complex mixture of cultures in Indonesia, kindly permitted me to read the manuscript of the book he had written upon the subject. With remarkable perspicuity he had unravelled the apparently hopeless tangle into which the social organisation of this ethnological cockpit has been involved by the mixture of peoples and the conflict of diverse beliefs and customs. His convincing demonstration of the fact that there had been an immigration into Indonesia (from the West) of a people who introduced megalithic ideas, sun-worship and phallism, and many other distinctive practices and traditions, not only gave me precisely the information I needed, but also directed my attention to the fact that the culture (for which, so he informed me, Professor Brockwell, of Montreal, had suggested the distinctive term "heliolithic") included also the practice of mummification. In the course of continuous discussions with him during the last four months a clear view of the whole problem and the means of solving most of its difficulties emerged.

For Perry's work in this field, no less than for my own, Rivers' illuminating and truly epoch-making researches (**64** to **70**) have cleared the ground. Not only has he removed from the path of investigators the apparently insuperable obstacles to the demonstration of the spread of cultures by showing how useful arts can be lost (**65**); but he has analysed the social organisation of Oceania in such a way that the various waves of immigration into the Pacific can be identified and with certainty be referred back to Indonesia (**69**). Many other scholars in the past have produced evidence (for example **2**; **60**; **61** and **98**) to demonstrate that the Polynesians came from Indonesia; but Rivers analysed and defined the characteristic features of several streams of culture which flowed from Indonesia into the Pacific. Perry undertook the task of tracing these peoples through the Indonesian maze and pushing back their origins to India. In the present communication I shall attempt to sketch in broad outline the process of the gradual accumulation in Egypt and the neighbourhood of the cultural outfit of these great wanderers, and to follow them in their migrations west, south and east from the place where their curious assortment of customs and accomplishments became fortuitously associated one with the other (*Map II.*).

I cannot claim that my colleagues in this campaign against what seems to us to be the utterly mistaken precepts of modern ethnology see altogether eye to eye with me. They have been dealing exclusively with more primitive peoples amongst whom every new attainment, in arts and crafts, in beliefs and social organisation, in everything in fact that we regard as an element of civilization, has been introduced from without by more cultured races, or fashioned in the conflict between races of different traditions and ideals.

My investigations, on the contrary, have been concerned mainly with the actual invention of the elements of civilization and with the people who created practically all of its ingredients—the ideas, the implements and methods of the arts and crafts which give expression to it. Though superficially my attitude may seem to clash with theirs, in that I am attempting to explain the primary origin of some of the things, with which they are dealing only as ready-made customs and beliefs that were handed on from people to people, there is no real antagonism between us.

It is obvious that there must be a limit to the application of the borrowing-explanation; and when we are forced to consider the people who really invented things, it is necessary to frame some working hypothesis in explanation of such achievements, unless we feebly confess that it is useless to attempt such enquiries.

In previous works (**82 and 85**) I have explained why it must be something more than a mere coincidence that in Egypt, where the operation of natural forces leads to the preservation of the corpse when buried in the hot dry sand, it should have become a cardinal tenet in the beliefs of the people to strive after the preservation of the body as the essential means of continuing an existence after death. When death occurred the only difference that could be detected between the corpse and the living body was the absence of the vital spirit from the former. [For the interpretation of the Egyptians' peculiar ideas concerning death, see Alan Gardiner's, important article (**23**).] It was in a condition in some sense analogous to sleep; and the corpse, therefore, was placed in its "dwelling" in the soil lying in the attitude naturally assumed, by primitive people when sleeping. Its vital spirit or *ka* was liberated from the body, but hovered round the corpse so long as its tissues were preserved. It needed food and all the other things that ministered to the welfare and comfort of the living, not omitting the luxuries and personal adornments which helped to make life pleasant. Hence at all times graves became the objects of plunder on the part of unscrupulous contemporaries; and so incidentally the knowledge was forthcoming from time to time of the fate of the body in the grave.

The burial customs of the Proto-Egyptians, starting from those common to the whole group of the Brown Race in the Neolithic phase, first became differentiated from the rest when special importance came to be attached to the preservation of the actual tissues of the body.

It was this development, no doubt, that prompted, their more careful arrangements for the protection of the corpse, and gradually led to the aggrandisement of the tomb, the more abundant provision of food offerings and funerary equipment in general.

Even in the earliest known Pre-dynastic period the Proto-Egyptians were in the habit of loosely wrapping their dead in linen—for the art of the weaver goes back to that remote time in Egypt—and then protecting the wrapped corpse from contact with the soil by an additional wrapping of goat-skin or matting.

Then, as the tomb became larger, to accommodate the more abundant offerings, almost every conceivable device was tried to protect the body from such contact. Instead of the goat-skin or matting, in many cases the same result was obtained by lining the grave with series of sticks, with slabs of wood, with pieces of unhewn stone, or by lining the grave with mud-bricks. In other cases, again, large pottery coffins, of an oblong, elliptical, or circular form, were used. Later on, when metal implements were invented (**90**), and the skill to use them created the crafts of the carpenter and stonemason, coffins of wood or stone came into vogue. It is quite certain that the coffin and sarcophagus were Egyptian inventions. The mere fact of this extraordinary variety of means and materials employed in Egypt, when in other countries one definite method was adopted, is proof of the most positive kind that these measures for lining the grave were actually invented in Egypt. For the inventor tries experiments: the borrower imitates one definite thing. During this process of gradual evolution, which occupied the whole of the Pre- and Proto-dynastic periods, the practice of inhumation (in the strict sense of the term) changed step by step into one of burial in a tomb. In other words, instead of burial in the soil, the body came to be lodged in a carefully constructed subterranean chamber, which no longer was filled up with earth. The further stages in this process of evolution of tomb construction, the way in which the rock-cut tomb came into existence, and the gradual development of the stone superstructure and temple of offerings—all of these matters have been summarised in some detail in my article on the evolution of megalithic monuments (**94**).

What especially I want to emphasize here is that in Egypt is preserved every stage in the gradual transformation of the burial customs from simple inhumation into that associated with the fully-developed rock-cut tomb and the stone temple. There can be no question that the craft of the stonemason and the practice of building megalithic monuments originated in Egypt. In addition, I want to make it quite clear that there is the most intimate genetic relationship between the development of these megalithic practices and the origin of the art of mummification.

For in course of time the early Egyptians came to learn, no doubt again from the discoveries of their tomb-robbers, that the fate of the corpse, after remaining for some time in a roomy rock-cut tomb or stone coffin, was vastly different from that which befell the body when simply buried in the hot, dry, desiccating sand. In respect of the former they acquired the idea which the Greeks many centuries later embalmed in the word "sarcophagus" under the simple belief that the disappearance of the flesh was due to the stone in some mysterious way devouring it.[7] [Certain modern archæologists within recent years have entertained an equally child-like, though even less informed, view when they claimed the absence of any trace of the flesh in certain stone sarcophagi as evidence in favour of a fantastic belief that the Neolithic people of the Mediterranean area were addicted to the supposed practice which Italian archæologists call *scarnitura*.]

But by the time the discovery was made that bodies placed in more sumptuous tombs were no longer preserved as they were apt to be when buried in the sand, the idea of the necessity for the preservation of the body as the essential condition for the attainment of a future existence had become fixed in the minds of the people and established by several centuries of belief as *the* cardinal tenet of their faith. Thus the very measures they had taken the more surely to guard and preserve the sacred remains of their dead had led to a result the reverse of what had been intended.

The elaborate ritual that had grown up and the imposing architectural traditions were not abandoned when this discovery was made. Even in these modern enlightened days human nature does not react in that way. The cherished beliefs held by centuries of ancestors are not renounced for any discovery of science. The ethnologist has not given up his objections to the idea of the spread of culture, now that all the difficulties that militated against the acceptance of the common-sense view have been removed! Nor did the Egyptians of the Proto-dynastic period revert to the practices of their early ancestors and take to sand-burial again. They adopted the only other alternative open to a people who retained implicitly the belief in the necessity of preserving the body, *i.e.*, they set about attempting to attain by art what nature unaided no longer secured, so long as they clung to their custom of burying in large tombs. They endeavoured artificially to preserve the bodies of their dead.

This explains what I meant to imply when I said that the megalithic idea and the incentive to mummify the dead are genetically related, the one to the other. The stone-tomb came into existence as a direct result of the importance attached to the corpse. This development defeated the very object that inspired it. The invention of the art of embalming was the logical outcome of the attempt to remedy this unexpected result.

As in the history of every similar happening elsewhere, necessity, or what these simple-minded people believed to be a necessity, was the "mother of invention."

In the course of the following discussion it will be seen that the practice of mummification became linked up in another way with what may be called the megalithic traditions. The crudely-preserved body no longer retained any likeness to the person as his friends knew him when alive. A life-like stone statue was therefore made to represent him. Magical means (p. 24) were adopted to give life to the statue. Thus originated the belief that a stone might become the dwell-

[7] It is a curious reflection that the idea of stone living which made such a fantastic belief possible may itself have arisen from the Egyptian practices about to be described.

ing of a living person; and that a person when dead may become converted into stone. So insistent did this belief become that among more uncultured people, who borrowed Egyptian practices but were unable to make portrait statues, a rudely-shaped or even unhewn pillar of stone came to be regarded as the dwelling of the deceased.

Thus from being the mere device for the identification of the deceased the stone statue degenerated among less cultured people into an object even less like the dead man than his own crudely-made mummy. But the fundamental idea remained and became the starting point for that rich crop of petrifaction-myths and beliefs concerning men and animals living in stones.

Thus arose in Egypt, somewhere about 3000 B.C., the nucleus of the "heliolithic" culture-complex—mummification, megalithic architecture, and the making of idols, three practices most intimately and genetically linked one with the other. But it was the merest accident that the people amongst whom these customs developed, should also have been weavers of linen, workers in copper, worshippers of the sun and serpent, and practitioners of massage and circumcision.

But it was not for another fifteen centuries that the characteristic "heliolithic" culture-complex was completed by the addition of numerous other trivial customs, like ear-piercing, tattooing and the use of the swastika, none of which originated in Egypt, but happened to have become "tacked on" to that distinctive culture before its great world tour began.

The earliest unquestionable evidence (**89**) of an attempt artificially to preserve the body was found in a rock-cut tomb of the Second Dynasty, at Sakkara. It is important to note that the body was lying in a *flexed* position upon the left side, and was contained in a short wooden coffin, modelled like a house. The limbs were wrapped separately and large quantities of fine linen bandages had been applied around all parts of the body, so as to mould the wrapped mummy to a life-like form.

Thus in the earliest mummy—or, to be strictly accurate, in the remains which exhibit the earliest evidence of the attempt at embalming—we find exemplified the two objects that the Ancient Egyptian embalmer aimed at throughout the whole history of his craft, viz., to preserve the actual tissues of the body, as well as the form and likeness of the deceased as he was when alive.

From the first the embalmer realised the limitations of his craftsmanship, *i.e.*, that he was unable to make the body itself life-like. Hence he strove to preserve its tissues and then to make use of its wrappings for the purpose of fashioning a model or statue of the dead man. At first this was done while the body was flexed in the traditional manner. But soon the flexed position was gradually abandoned. Perhaps this change was brought about because it was easier to model the superficial form of a wrapped body when extended; and the greater success of the results so obtained may have been sufficiently important to have outweighed the restraining influence of tradition. The change may have occurred all the more readily at this time as beds were coming into use, and the idea of placing the "sleeping" body on a bed may have helped towards the process of extension.

But whatever view is taken of the explanation of the change of the attitude of the body, it is certain that it began soon after the first attempts at mummification were made. The evidence of extended burials, referred to the First Dynasty, which were found by Flinders Petrie at Tarkhan (**54**), may seem to contradict this: but there are reasons for believing that attempts at embalming were being made even at that time (**85**). It seems to be definitely proved that this change was not due to any foreign influence (**45**). At the time that it occurred there was a very considerable alien element in the population of Egypt; but the admixture took place long before the change in the position of the body was manifested. Perhaps the presence of a large foreign element may have weakened the sway of Egyptian tradition; but the evidence seems definitely opposed to the inference that it played any active part in the change of custom. For the history of the gradual way in which the change was slowly effected is certain proof of the causal factors at work. There was no sudden adoption of the fully extended position, but a slow and very gradual straightening of the limbs—a process which it took centuries to complete. The analysis of the evidence by Mace is quite conclusive on this point (**45**).

I am strongly of the opinion that there is a causal relationship between this gradual extension of the body and the measures for the reconstruction of a life-like model of the deceased, with the help of the mummy's wrappings. In other words, the adoption of the extended position was a direct result of the introduction of mummification.

At an early stage in the history of these changes it seems to have been realised that the likeness of the deceased which could be made of the wrapped mummy lacked the exactness and precision demanded of a portrait Perhaps also there may have been some doubt as to the durability of a statue made of linen.

A number of interesting developments occurred at about this time to overcome these defects. In one case (**85**), found at Mêdum by Flinders Petrie, the superficial bandages were saturated with a paste of resin and soda, and the same material was applied to the surface of the wrappings, which, while still in a plastic condition, was very skilfully moulded to form a life-like statue. The resinous carapace thus built up set to form a covering of stony hardness. Special care was devoted to the modelling of the head (sometimes the face only) and the genitalia, no doubt to serve as the means of identifying the individual and indicating the sex respectively.

The hair (or, perhaps, it would be more correct to say, the wig) and the moustache were painted with a dark brown or black resinous mixture, and the pupils, eyelids and eyebrows were represented by painting with a mixture of malachite powder and resinous paste. In other cases, recently described by Junker (**40**), plaster was used for the same purpose as the resinous paste in Petrie's mummy. In two of the four instances of this practice found by Junker, only the head was modelled.

The special importance assigned to the head is one of the outstanding features of ancient Egyptian statuary. It was exemplified in another way in the tombs of the early part of the Old Kingdom, as Junker has recalled in his memoir, by the construction of stone portrait-statues of the head only, which were made life-size and placed in the burial chamber alongside the mummy. It seems to me that Junker overlooks an essential, if not the, chief, reason for the special importance assigned to the head when he attributes it to the fact that the head contained the organs of sight, smell, hearing and taste. There can be no doubt that the head was modelled because it affords the chief means of recognising an individual. This portrayal of the features enabled any one, including the deceased's own *ka*, to identify the owner. Every circumstance of the making and the use of these heads bears out this interpretation, and no one has explained these facts more lucidly than Junker himself.

[Since the foregoing paragraphs have been put into print a preliminary report has come to hand from Professor Reisner, to whom I am indebted for most of my information regarding these portrait heads—*Museum of Fine Arts Bulletin*, Boston, April, 1915.]

At a somewhat later period in the Old Kingdom the making of these so-called "substitution-heads" was discontinued, and it became the practice to make a statue of the whole man (of woman), which was placed above-ground in the megalithic *serdab* within the *mastaba* (see **94**). But even when the complete statue was made for the *serdab* the head alone was the part that was modelled with any approach to realism. In other words, the importance of the head as the chief means of identification was still recognised. Moreover, this idea manifested itself throughout the whole history of Egyptian mummification, for as late as the first century of the Christian era a portrait of the deceased was placed in front of the face of the mummy.

Thus in course of time the original idea of converting the wrapped body itself into a portrait-statue of the deceased was temporarily[8] abandoned and the mummy was stowed away in the burial chamber at the bottom of a deep shaft, the better to protect it from desecration, while the portrait-statue was placed above ground, in a strong chamber (*serdab*), hidden in the *mastaba* (**94**).

A certain magical value soon came to be attached to the statue in the *serdab*. It provided the body in which the *ka* could become reincarnated, and the deceased, thus reconstituted by magical means, could pass through the small hole in the *serdab* to enter the chapel of offerings and enjoy the food and the society of his friends there.

Dr. Alan Gardiner has kindly given me the following note in reference to this matter: "That statues in Egypt were meant to be efficient animate substitutes for the person or creature they portrayed has not been sufficiently emphasised hitherto. Over every statue or image were performed the rites of 'opening the mouth'—magical passes made with a kind of metal chisel in front of the mouth. Besides the *up-ro* 'mouth opening,' other words testify to the prevalence of the same idea; the word for 'to fashion' a statue (*ms*) is to all appearances identical with *ms* 'to give birth,' and the term for the sculptor was *sa 'nkh*, 'he who causes to live.'"

---

[8] How insistent the desire was to make a statue of the mummy itself is shown by the repeated attempts made in later times; see the account of the mummies of Amenophis III. (**86**) and of the rulers and priests of the XXIst and XXIInd Dynasties (**78** and **87**).

As Blackman (5) has pointed out, the Pyramid Texts make it clear that libations were poured out and incense burnt before the statue or the mummy with the specific object of restoring to it the moisture and the odour respectively which the body had during life.

I have already indicated how, out of the conception of the possibility of bringing to life the stone portrait-statue, a series of curious customs were developed. Among peoples on a lower cultural plane, who were less skilled than the Egyptians in stone-carving, the making of a life-like statue was beyond their powers. Sometimes they made the attempt to represent the human form; in other cases crude representations of the breasts or suggestions of the genitalia were the only signs on a stone pillar to indicate that it was meant to represent a human statue: in many cases a simple uncarved block of stone was set up. But the idea that such a pillar, whether carved or not, was the dwelling of some deceased person, seized the imagination and spread far and wide. It is seen in the Pygmalion and Galatea story, and its converse in the tragic history of Lot's wife. It is found throughout the Mediterranean area, the whole littoral of Southern Asia, Indonesia, the Pacific Islands and America, and can be regarded as definite evidence of the influence of the cult that developed in association with the practice of mummification.

It is necessary to emphasise that the making of portrait-statues was an outcome of the practice of mummification and an integral part of the cult associated with that burial custom. Hartland falls into grave error when he writes "where other peoples set up images of the deceased, those who practised desiccation or embalmment were enabled to keep the bodies themselves" (32, p. 418). It was precisely the people who embalmed or preserved the bodies of their dead who also made statues of them.

As these stones, according to such beliefs, could be made to hear and speak (23), they naturally became oracles. People were able to commune with and get advice and instruction from the kings and wise men who dwelt within these stone pillars. Thus it became the custom in many lands for meetings of special solemnity, such as those where important decisions had to be made, to be held at stone circles, where the members of the convention sat on the stones and communed with their ancestors, former rulers or wise men, who dwelt in the stones (or the grave) in the centre of the circle.

"Chardin, in his account of the stone circles he saw in Persia, mentions a tradition that they were used as places of assembly, each member of the council being seated on a stone; Homer, in his description of the shield of Achilles in the *Iliad*, speaks of the elders sitting in the place of justice upon stones in a circle; Plot, in his account of the Rollrich stones in Oxfordshire, says that Olaus Wormius, Saxo Grammaticus, Meursius, and many other early historians, concur in stating that it was the practice of the ancient Danes to elect their kings in stone circles, each member of the council being seated upon a stone; the tradition arising out of this custom, that these stones represent petrified giants, is widely spread in all countries where they occur, and Col. Forbes Leslie has shown that within the historic period, these circles were used in Scotland as places of justice" (Lane Fox, (20), p. 64). Is not our king crowned seated upon the Lia-fail, which is now in the coronation chair at Westminster? Such customs and beliefs are widespread also in India, Indonesia, and beyond, as W. J. Perry has pointed out. The practices still observed in the Khasia Hills in modern times clearly indicate the significance of this use of stone seats; and the custom can be found from the Canary Islands in the West (**26**) to Costa Rica in the East, encircling the whole globe (compare *"Man,"* May, 1915, p. 79).

I shall enter more fully into the consideration of the origin of the ideas associated with stone seats when Perry has published his important analysis of the significance of so curious a practice.

The converse of the belief in the bringing to life of stone statues—or perhaps it would be more correct to say, the complementary view that, if a stone can be converted into a living creature, the latter can also be transformed into stone—is found also wherever the parent belief is known to exist. As a rule it forms part of a complexly interwoven series of traditions concerning the creation, the deluge, the destruction of the "sons of men" by petrifaction, and the repeopling the earth by the incestuous intercourse of the "children of the gods."

Perry, who has made a study of the geographical distribution and associations of these curiously-linked traditions, has clearly demonstrated that they form an integral part of the cultural equipment of the sun-worshipping, stone-using peoples.

In the foregoing statement I have endeavoured to indicate also their genetic connection with the ideas that sprang from the early practice of mummification in Egypt.

There are many other curious features of the early Egyptian practices which might have served as straws to indicate how the cultural current had flowed, if much more substantial proofs had not been available of the reality of the movement. The diffusion of such a distinctive object as the Egyptian head-rest, which used to be buried with mummies of the Pyramid Age, is an example. It occurs widely spread in Africa, Southern Asia, Indonesia and the Pacific.

But the use of beds as funerary biers is a much more distinctive custom. The believers in theories of the independent evolution of customs may say "is it not natural to expect that people who regarded death as a kind of sleep should have placed head-rests and beds in the graves of their dead?" But how would such ethnologists explain the use of a funerary bier on the part of people (such as many of the less cultured people who adopted this Egyptian custom) who do not themselves use beds?

The evidence afforded by the use of biers is, in fact, a most definite demonstration of the diffusion of customs. Although it is a familiar scene in ancient Egyptian pictures to find the mummy borne upon a bed—a custom which we know from Egyptian literature, no less than that of the Jews, Phœnicians, Greeks and Romans to have been actually observed—only one Egyptian cemetery, so far as I am aware—a proto-dynastic site, excavated by Flinders Petrie (**54**) at Tarkhan—has revealed corpses lying upon beds. But in a cemetery, some sixteen centuries later, excavated by Reisner in the Soudan (**62**), a similar practice was demonstrated. Garstang has recorded the observance of a similar custom further South (Meroe) at a later date.

These form useful connecting links with the region around the head-waters of the Nile, where even in modern times this practice has survived, and the mummified corpse of the king is placed upon a rough bier. I shall have occasion to point out later on that this curious practice spread from East Africa along the Asiatic littoral to Indonesia, Melanesia and Polynesia, thence to the American continent; and in most places was definitely associated with attempts at preservation of the corpse.

In many places along the whole course of the same great track, instead of a bed, a boat of some sort, usually a rough dug-out, was used. This practice also was observed in Egypt, where its symbolic purpose is clearly apparent.

Another distinctive feature of the burial customs in the same area was the idea that the grave represented the house in which the deceased was sleeping. How definitely this view was held by the proto-Egyptians is seen in their coffins, subterranean burial chambers, and the superstructures of their tombs, all three of which were originally represented as dwelling houses (see my memoir, **94**).

The Pyramid texts clearly explain the precise significance and origin of the hitherto mysterious and widespread custom of burning incense at the statue. For, as Blackman (**5**) has pointed out, the aim was by burning aromatic woods and resins thereby magically to restore to the "body" the odours of the living person.

It was therefore intimately related to the practice of mummification and genetically connected with it. It was part of the magical procedure for making the portrait-statue of the deceased (or later, in the time of the New Empire, the mummy itself) "an efficient animate substitute for the person" (Alan Gardiner).

A careful investigation of the geographical distribution of the custom of burning incense before the corpse and of the circumstances related to such a practice has convinced me that wherever it is found, even where no attempt is made to preserve the body, it can be regarded as an indication of the influence of the Egyptian custom of mummification. For apart from such an influence incense-burning is inexplicable. The attempt on the part of certain writers to explain the use of incense merely as a means of disguising the odours of putrefaction will not bear examination. It is an example of that kind of so-called psychological explanation which is opposed by all the ascertainable facts.

Beyond the borders of Egypt peoples who for a time adopted the custom of embalming and then for some reason, such as the failure to attain successful results or the adoption of conflicting beliefs or customs, allowed the practice to lapse, the simpler parts of the Egyptian funerary ritual often continued to be observed. The body was anointed with oil, perhaps packed in salt and aromatic plants, wrapped in linen or fine clothes, had incense burned before it, and was laid on a bed or special bier. All of these practices originated in Egypt and observance of any or all of them is to be regarded as a sure sign of the influence of the Egyptian custom of mummification. Among the more immediate neighbours of the Egyptians, such as the Jews, Greeks and Romans, the evidence for this is clear. Occasionally the full process of embalming was followed, even if it were only a temporary procedure preliminary to the observance of some other burial custom, such as cremation, perhaps inspired by ideas wholly foreign to those which prompted mummification. I need not enumerate instances of this curious syncretism of burial customs, numerous examples of which will be found in Reutter (**63**, pp. 144-147) and in Hastings' Dictionary (**32**), as well as in the following pages.

At the very earliest period in Egypt from which historical records have come down to us (the time of the First Dynasty, 3200 B.C., or even earlier) "the king's favourite title was 'Horus,' by which he identified himself as the successor of the great god [the hawk sun-god] who had once ruled over the kingdom ... [other symbols often appeared] side by side with Buto, the serpent-goddess of the northern capital. As [the king] felt himself still as primarily king of Upper Egypt, it was not until later that he wore the serpent of the North, the sacred uraeus, upon his forehead." (Breasted, **6**, p. 38). "The sun-disc, with the outspread wings of the hawk, became the commonest symbol of their religion" (p. 54). But in the time of the Fourth Dynasty "the priests of Heliopolis now demanded that [the king, who had always been represented as the successor of the sun-god and had borne the title 'Horus'] be the bodily son of Ré, who henceforth would appear on earth to become the father of the Pharaoh" (p. 122).

Now, when the Pharaoh thus became identified with the great sun-god Ré, his Pyramid-temple became the place of worship of the sun-god. Megalithic architecture thus became indissolubly connected with sun-worship, simply from the accident of the invention of the art of building in stone—of erecting stone tombs, which were also temples of offerings—by a people who happened to be sun-worshippers and whose ruler's tomb became the shrine of the sun-god. I have already explained the close genetic connection between the practice of mummification and megalithic building.

The fact that the dominance of the sun-god Ré was attained in the northern capital, which was also the seat of serpent-worship, led to the association of the sun and the serpent.[9] From this purely fortuitous blending of the sun's disc with the uraeus, often combined, especially in later times, with the wings of the Horus-hawk, a symbolism came into being which was destined to spread until it encircled the world, from Ireland to America. For an excellent example of this composite symbolism from America see Bancroft, (**3**), Vol. IV., p. 351. A more striking illustration of the completeness of the transference of a complex and wholly artificial design from Ancient Egypt to America could not be imagined. [For the full discussion of the original association of the sun and the serpent see Sethe's important *Memoir* (**74**).]

The chance circumstances which led to the linking together of all these incongruous elements—mummification, megalithic architecture, the idea of the king as son of the sun, sun and serpent worship and its curious symbolism—were created in Egypt, so that, wherever these peculiar customs or traditions make their appearance elsewhere in association the one with the other, it can confidently be

---

[9] For an account of the geographical distribution of serpent-worship and a remarkable demonstration of the intimacy of its association with distinctive "heliolithic" ideas, see Wake (**103**).

regarded as a sure token of Egyptian influence, exerted directly or indirectly.

When certain modern ethnologists argue that it is the most natural thing in the world for primitive peoples to worship the sun as the obvious source of warmth and fertility, and therefore such worship can have no value as an indication of the contact of peoples, on general principles one might be prepared to admit the validity of the claim. But when it is realised that sun-worship, wherever it is found, is invariably associated with part (or the whole) of a large series of curiously incongruous customs and beliefs, it is no longer possible to regard the worship of the sun as having originated independently in several centres. Why should the sun-worshipper also worship the serpent and use a winged symbol, build megalithic monuments, mummify his dead, and practise a large series of fantastic tricks to which other peoples are not addicted? There is no inherent reason why a man who worships the sun should also tattoo his face, perforate his ears, practise circumcision, and make use of massage. In fact, until the time of the New Empire, the sun-worshipping Egyptian did not practise ear-piercing and tattooing, thereby illustrating the fact that originally these practices were not part of the cult, and that their eventual association with it was purely accidental. This only serves more definitely to confirm the view that it was the fortuitous association of a curious series of customs in Egypt at the time of the New Empire which supplied the cultural outfit of the "heliolithic" wanderers for their great migration.

In accordance with Egyptian beliefs "the sun was born every morning and sailed across the sky in a celestial barque, to arrive in the west and descend as an old man tottering into the grave" (Breasted, (**6**), p. 54).

The deceased might reach the west by being borne across in the sun-god's barque: friendly spirits, the four sons of Horus, might bring him a craft on which he might float over: but by far the majority depended upon the services of a ferryman called "Turnface" (Breasted, p. 65).

In later times (Middle Kingdom) a model boat, fully equipped, was usually put in the tomb, "in order that the deceased might have no difficulty in crossing the waters to the happy isles." "By the pyramid of Sesostris III., in the sands of the desert, there were even buried five large Nile boats, intended to carry the king and his house across these waters" (Breasted, p. 176).

At a later period "the triumph of a Theban family brought with it the supremacy of Amon.... His essential character and individuality had already been obliterated by the solar theology of the Middle Kingdom, when he had become Amon-Re, and with some attributes borrowed from his ithyphallic neighbour, Min of Coptos, he now rose to a unique and supreme position of unprecedented splendour" (6, p. 248). Thus there was added to this "heliolithic" complex of ideas the definitely phallic element: but one must confess that this aspect of the culture did not become obtrusive until it was planted in alien lands, where among the Phœnicians and the peoples of India the phallic aspect became more strongly emphasised. From time to time various writers have striven to demonstrate a phallic motive in almost every element of the culture now under consideration. What I want to make clear is that it was a late addition, which was relatively insignificant in the original home of the culture.

After this digression I must now return to the further consideration of the mummies themselves.

Direct examination of the mummified bodies does not, of course, afford any certain evidence of the application of oil or fat to the surface of the body. Large quantities of fatty material were often found in the mouth and the body cavity (**78**; **81** and **86**); and the surface of the body was often greasy; but, of course, the fatty materials in the skin itself might have afforded a sufficient explanation of this. Dr. Alan Gardiner, however, tells me that ancient Egyptian literature contains repeated references to the process of anointing the body with "oil of cedar,"[10] and great stress is laid upon this procedure as an essential element of the technique of embalming.[11]

Thus in the time of the decadence of the New Empire an Egyptian writer laments the loosening of Egypt's hold on the Lebanons, because if no "oil of cedar" were obtainable it might become impossible any longer to embalm the dead.

Diodorus Siculus, writing many centuries later, says the body was "anointed with oil of cedar and other things for thirty days, and afterwards with myrrh, cinnamon, and other such like matters" (Pettigrew, **56**, p. 62). Thus there can be little doubt that it was an essential part of the Ancient Egyptian technique to anoint the body with oil.

Pettigrew (**56**, p. 62, and also p. 242) adduces cogent reasons in proof of the fact that the Egyptians (and in modern times the Capuchins, at Palermo) made use of heat to desiccate the body, probably in a stove.

It is quite clear, therefore, that the Ancient Egyptians realised the importance of desiccation as an essential element in the preservation of the body. Moreover, they were familiar with a number of different means of ensuring this end:—(1) by burial in dry sand; (2) by exposure to the sun's rays; (3) by removing all the softer and more putrescible parts of the body; (4) possibly by massaging and squeezing out the juices from the body; (5) by the free use of alcohol (palm wine) and large quantities of powdered wood; and (6) by the aid of fire.

Dr. Alan Gardiner tells me that the most ancient Egyptian writings, such, for example, as the Pyramid texts, afford positive evidence that the Egyptians recognised the fact of the desiccation of the body in the process of embalming, for their scribes tell us, in the most definite manner, that the aim of the ceremony of

---

[10] Sir William Thiselton Dyer informs me that in all probability it was not *cedar* but *juniper* that was obtained by the Ancient Egyptians from Syria [and used for embalming]. The material to which reference is made here would probably be identical with the modern 'huile de cade,' and be obtained from *juniperus excelsa*.

I retain the term "oil of cedar" to facilitate the bibliographical references, as all the archæologists and historians invariably use this expression.

[11] Since this memoir has been printed Dr. Alan Gardiner has published a most luminous and important account of "The Tomb of Amenemhēt" (N. de Garis Davies and Alan Gardiner, 1915), which throws a flood of light upon Egyptian ideas concerning the matters discussed in this communication.

offering libations was magically to restore to the body (as represented by the statue above ground) the fluids it had lost during embalming (Blackman, **5**).

If then the Egyptians of the Pyramid Age recognised the importance of restoring the fluids to reanimate the mummy or its statue, it is quite clear they must have appreciated the physical fact that their process of preservation was largely a matter of desiccation.

It is a point of some interest and importance to note in this connection that the essential processes of mummification—(1) salting, (2) evisceration, (3) drying, and (4) smoking (or even cooking)—are identical with those adopted for the preservation of meat, and (5) the use of honey is analogous to the means taken to preserve fruit. In fact, the term used by Herodotus for the first stage of the Egyptian process of mummification is the term used for salting fish. It would be instructive to enquire in what measure these two needs of primitive man in North-East Africa mutually influenced one another, and led to an acquisition of knowledge useful to them for the preservation both of their food and their dead relatives!

To the constituent elements of the "heliolithic" culture may now be added the practices of anointing with oil or unguents, the burning of incense and the offering of libations, all derived from the ritual of embalming.

In considering the southern extension of Egyptian influence it must be remembered that as early "as 2600 B.C. the Egyptian had already begun the exploitation of the Upper Nile and had been led in military force as far as the present Province of Dongola" (**62**, p. 23). For several centuries Nubia and the Soudan were left very much to themselves. Then during the time of the Middle Kingdom Egypt once more exerted a powerful influence to the South. At the close of that period Egypt was overrun by the Hyksos.

At Kerma, near the Third Cataract, Reisner has recently unearthed a cemetery which he refers to the Hyksos Period (**62**, p. 23). "The burial customs are revolting in their barbarity. On a carved bed in the middle of a big circular pit the chief personage lies on his right side with his head east. Under his head is a wooden pillow: between his legs a sword or dagger. Around the bed lie a varying number of bodies, male and female, all contracted on the right side, head east. Among them are the pots and pans, the cosmetic jars, the stools, and other objects. Over the whole burial is spread a great ox-hide. It is clear they were all buried at once. The men and women round about must have been sacrificed so that their spirits might accompany the chief to the other world.... I could not escape the belief that they had been buried alive" (**62**). These funerary practices supply a most important link in the chain which I am endeavouring to forge. I would especially call attention (1) to the fact of the sacrifice of the chief's (? wives and) servants and (2) to the burial of the chief himself on a bed.

We know that the Egyptian practice of mummification spread south into Nubia (**39**) and the Soudan.

According to Herodotus the ancient Macrobioi preserved the bodies of their dead by drying: then they covered them with plaster, painted them to look like living men, and set them up in their houses for a year. For a fuller account of this practice and much more instructive information for comparison see Ridgeway's "Early Age of Greece," Vol. I., p. 483 *et seq.*

Numerous references in the classical writers lead us to believe that a similar custom of keeping the mummy in the house of the relatives for a longer or shorter period may have been in vogue in Egypt. Throughout the widespread area in which mummification was practised—from Africa to America—a precisely similar practice is found among many peoples.

The custom of covering the mummies with plaster[12] is an interesting survival of the practice described by Junker in Egypt (*vide supra*), which seems to supply the explanation of the curious measures adopted for modelling the face in Melanesia.

Even at the present day, centuries after the art of the embalmer disappeared from Egypt, mummification is being attempted by certain people dwelling in the neighbourhood of the head-waters of the Nile.

In his article in Hastings' Dictionary (**32**, p. 418) Hartland states that the practice of mummification is found "more or less throughout the west of Africa: among the Niamniam of the Upper Nile basin the bodies of chiefs, and among the Baganda the kings, are preserved, and the custom is found also among the Warundi in German East Africa (Frobenius); and in British Central Africa the corpse is rubbed with boiled maize (Werner)."

Roscoe (**72**, p. 105), in his book on the Baganda, describes the process of embalming the king's body. As in Egypt, the body was disembowelled; and the bowels were washed in beer, just as the Egyptians, according to Herodotus and Diodorus, are said to have done with palm-wine. The viscera were spread out in the sun to dry and were then returned to the body, as was done in Egypt at the time of the XXIst Dynasty. The body was then dried and washed with beer.

So far as we are aware, the Egyptians never sacrificed any human beings at their funerals, although they often placed in the *serdab* of the *mastaba* statues of the deceased's wife, family and servants, to ensure him their presence and the comforts of a home in his new form of existence.

In the quotations from Reisner's report, it has just been seen that he found some burials made about 1800 B.C., in which servants appear to have been sacrificed.

In the case of the Baganda, Roscoe describes the killing of the king's wives and attendants at his funeral.

Roscoe further describes (in his book) the body of the chief as being laid on a bed or framework of plantain trees (p. 117).

At the end of five months the head was removed from the mummy and the jaw-bone was removed, cleaned, and then buried, and a large conical thatched

---

[12] Mr. Crooke has called my attention to a similar practice in India. Leith (Journ. Anthr. Soc. of Bombay, Vol. I., 1886, pp. 39 and 40) stated that the *Káší Khanda* contained an account of a Bráhman who preserved his mother's corpse. After having it preserved and wrapped he "coated the whole with pure clay and finally deposited the corpse in a copper coffin."

temple was built over the jaw. [In the islands of the Torres Straits the same curious custom of rescuing the head after about six months is also found; but it was the tongue and not the jaw which received special attention (**25** and **27**)].

In Egypt, where the practice of mummification was most successful, special treatment of the head was not necessary, except occasionally in Ptolemaic times (**39**), when carelessness on the part of the embalmer led to disastrous results and it became necessary to "fake" a body for attachment to the separated head. But as the Baganda were unable to make a mummy which would last, they adopted these special measures with regard to the skull. Originally special importance was attached to the head, primarily (*vide supra*) as a means of identifying the deceased. But when the practice of preservation spread to uncultured people, whose efforts at embalming were ineffectual, the idea was transferred to the skull, the reason for the special treatment of the head probably being forgotten. Why such peculiar honour should be devoted to the jaw can only be surmised from our knowledge of the belief that the deceased was supposed to be able to talk and communicate with the living (**21**).

In his article in the *Journal of the Anthropological Institute* (**72**, p. 44) Roscoe give some further particulars. Four men and four women were clubbed to death at the funeral ceremony of the king.

The body was wrapped in strips of bark cloth and each finger and toe was wrapped separately.

In *L'Anthropologie* (T. 21, 1910, p. 53) Poutrin says of the burial customs of the M'Baka people of French Congo "le corps, préalablement embaumé avec des herbes sécher et de la cendre est couché sur un lit."

Weeks (**104**, pp. 450 and 451) gives an account of the burial customs of the Bangala of the Upper Congo. "They took out the entrails and buried them, placed the corpse on a frame, lit a fire under it, and thoroughly smoke-dried it." "The dried body was tied in a mat, put in a roughly made hut." "Coffins were often made out of old canoes." "Poorer folk were rubbed with oil and red camwood powder, bound round with cloth and tied up in a mat."

One of the most remarkable instances of the survival of burial practices strangely reminiscent of those of ancient Egypt has been described by Mr. Amaury Talbot (**99**). Among the Ibibio people living in the extreme south-west corner of Nigeria, bordering on the Gulf of Guinea, he found that both the Ibibios and a neighbouring tribe, the Ibos, had burial rites which "recall those of ancient Egypt." For instance, "among Ibos embalming is still practised." Two methods of mummification, in which the evisceration of the corpse takes place, are practised.

For the grave "a wide-mouthed pit" was dug and "from the bottom of this an underground passage, sometimes thirty feet long, led into a square chamber with no other outlet. In this the dead body was laid, and, after the bearers had returned to the light of day, stones were set over the pit mouth and earth strewn over all." Further, in the case of the Ibibios, "in some prominent spot near the town arbour-like erections are raised as memorials, and furnished with the favourite property of the dead man. At the back or side of these is placed what we always called a little 'Ka' house, with window or door, into the central chamber, provided, as in ancient Egypt, for the abode of the dead man's Ka or double. Figures of the Chief, with favourite wives and slaves, may also be seen—counterparts of the Ushabtiu."

From the photographs illustrating Mr. Talbot's article many other remarkable points of resemblance to ancient Egyptian practices are to be noted.

The snake and the sun constitute the obtrusive features of the crude design painted in the funeral shrine. The fact that so many features of the Egyptian burial practices should have been retained (and in association with many other elements of the "heliolithic" culture) in this distant spot, on the other side of the continent, raises the question whether or not its proximity to the Atlantic littoral may not be a contributory factor in the survival. They may have been spared by the remoteness of the retreat and the relative freedom from disturbance, to which nearer localities in the heart of the continent may have been subjected. But, on the other hand, there is the possibility that the spread of culture around the coast may have brought these Egyptian practices to Old Calabar. In the next few pages it will be seen that such a possibility is not so unlikely as it may appear at first sight.

But the fact that it was the custom among the Ibibio to bury the wives of the king with his mummy suggests a truly African, as distinct from purely Egyptian, influence, and makes it probable that the custom spread across the continent. This view is further supported by the traditions of the people themselves, no less than by the physical features of their crania (see *Report British Association*, 1912, p. 613).

As the people of the Ivory Coast (*vide infra*) practice a method of embalming which is clearly Egyptian and untainted by these African influences, it is clear that the two streams of Nilotic culture, one across the continent *viâ* Kordofan and Lake Chad and the other around the coasts of the Mediterranean and Atlantic, after reaching the West Coast must have met somewhere between the mouth of the Niger and the Ivory Coast.

[Since writing the above paragraphs, in which inferences as to racial movements across Africa were based solely upon the distribution and methods of mummification, I have become acquainted with remarkable confirmation of these views from two different sources. Frobenius, in his book "The Voice of Africa," 1913 (see especially the map on p. 449, Vol. II.), makes an identical delimitation of the two spheres of influence from the east, trans- and circum-African (*i.e.*, *viâ* the Mediterranean) respectively.

Sir Harry Johnston ("A Survey of the Ethnography of Africa," *Journ. Roy. Anthr. Inst.*, 1913, p. 384) supplies even more precise and definite confirmation of the route taken by the Egyptian culture-migration across Kordofan to Lake Chad, thence to the Niger basin and "all parts of West Africa."

He adds further (pp. 412 and 413):—"Stone worship and the use of stone in building and sepulture extend from North Africa southwards across the desert region to Senegambia (sporadically) and the northern parts of the Sudan, and to Somaliland. The superstitious use of stone in connection with religion, burial and after-death memorial, reappears again in Yoruba, in the North-West Cameroons and adjoining Calabar region (Ekir-land).″]

For the purpose of embalming the bodies of their dead "the Baoule of the Ivory Coast remove the intestines, wash them with palm wine or European alcohol, introduce alcohol and salt into the body cavity, afterwards replacing the intestines and stitching up the opening." (Clozel and Villamur, quoted by Hartland, (**32**), p. 418.)

Scattered around the western shores of the African continent there are numerous ethnological features to suggest that it has been subjected to the influence of the megalithic culture spreading from the Mediterranean. But there is no spot in which this influence and its Egyptian derivation is more definitely and surely demonstrated than in the Canary Islands.

For the art of embalming was practised there in the truly Egyptian fashion; and it became a matter of some interest to discover whether or not the Nigerian customs were influenced in any way by the Guanche practices.

There can be little doubt that the practices on the Ivory Coast, to which reference has just been made, were either inspired by the Guanches or by the same influence which started embalming in the Canary Islands.

The information we possess in reference to the Canary Islands was collected by Bory de Saint Vincent ("Les Îles Fortunées," 1811, p. 54) and has been summarized by many writers, especially Pettigrew, Haigh and Reutter.

From Miss Haigh's account (**26**, p. 112) I make the following extracts: —

"When any person died they preserved the body in this manner; first, they carried it to a cave and stretched it on a flat stone, opened it and took out the bowels; then twice a day they washed the porous parts of the body with salt and water; afterwards they anointed it with a composition of sheep's butter mixed with a powder made from the dust of decayed pine trees, and a sort of brushwood called "Bressos," together with powdered pumice stone, and then dried it in the sun for fifteen days....

"When the body was thoroughly dried, and had become very light, it was wrapped in sheep skins or goat skins, girded tight with long leather thongs, and carried to one of the sepulchral grottoes, usually situated in the most inaccessible parts of the island.

"The bodies were either upright against the sides of the cavern, or side by side upon a kind of scaffolding made of branches of juniper, mocan, or other incorruptible wood.

"The knives for opening the body were made of sharp pieces of obsidian.

"In the grotto of Tacoronté was the mummy of an old woman dried in the sitting posture like that of the Peruvian corpses."

The mummies were wrapped in reddish goat skin, just as the shroud of Egyptian mummies was often of red linen.

From the same article, in which, as the above quotation states, the body was placed upon a stone for the purpose of the embalmer's operations, I should like to call attention to the following statement of a curious custom which is found in the most diverse parts of the world, in most cases in association with the practice of mummification.

Tradition says that at his installation the new Mencey (or chief of a principality) is required to seat himself on a stone, cut in the form of a chair and covered with skins: one of his nearest relatives presents him with a sacred relic—the bone of the right arm of the chief of the reigning family (p. 60). I have already (*supra*) indicated the significance of this characteristic feature of the "heliolithic" culture.

Reutter (**63**) gives some additional information in reference to Guanche embalming. The incision was made in the lower part of the abdomen (in the flank). After the body had been treated with a saturated salt solution, the viscera were returned to the body. The orifices of the nose, mouth and eyes were "stopped with bitumen as was the Egyptian practice." After packing the cavities of the body with aromatic plants the body was exposed either to the sun, or in a stove, to desiccate it.

During this operation, other embalmers repeatedly smeared the body with a kind of ointment, prepared by mixing certain fats, with powdered odoriferous plants, resin, pumice stone and absorbent substances (p. 139).

As in Egypt, according to Herodotus and Diodorus,—and my own observations have verified their account, at any rate so far as its chief feature is concerned—there was another method of embalming in which no abdominal incision was made, unless it was per rectum.

When this cheaper method was employed the corpse was dried in the sun and some corrosive liquid, called "cedria" in the case of the Egyptians, but in that of the Guanches supposed by Dr. Parcelly to be Euphorbia juice, was injected for the purpose of dissolving the intestines and thus facilitating the process of preservation by removing the chief seat of decomposition.

[It is important to recall the fact, to which I have already referred in this account, that in the islands of the Torres Straits also the same two alternative methods of evisceration, either through a flank incision or per rectum were in use.]

Most mummies, wrapped in goat skins, were buried in caves. But those of kings and princes were placed in coffins cut out of a solid log, and buried (head north) in the open, a monument of pyramidal form being erected above them.

It is important to bear in mind that both in East and West Africa and in the Canary Islands the technical procedures in the practice of mummification are those which were not adopted in Egypt until the time of the XXIst Dynasty. I have already called attention to this fact in my references to the Torres Straits mummies (*vide supra*), and to the inference that these extensive migrations of Egyptian influence could not have begun before the ninth century B.C.

(For more complete bibliographical references, see Pettigrew, (**56**), p. 233.)

The large series of identical procedures makes it absolutely certain that the method of embalming practised in the Canary Islands was derived from Egypt, and not earlier than 900 B.C.

Reutter states (**63**, p. 137) that "the Carthaginians, as the result of long-continued commercial intercourse with Egypt, assimilated its civilization even to the extent of worshipping certain of the Egyptian gods and of accepting many of her ideas and beliefs as to a future life."

"These reasons impelled them to practise the art of embalming and to represent the features of the dead upon their sarcophagi to enable the soul to refind its double."

"Their burial chambers, for the most part not built up, but carved out of the rock, communicated with the exterior by a staircase. Above them were built mastabas or monuments to be utilised, as amongst the Egyptians, as offering-places" (p. 138).

"Even the inscriptions in the mortuary chambers were written in hieroglyphics, and their sarcophagi contained scarabs inscribed with invocations to the Egyptian gods, Ptah, Bes and Ra, &c."

This reference is sufficient to indicate how the later (certainly not earlier than 900 B.C. and probably some centuries later) Egyptian practices spread around the Mediterranean.

I do not propose (in the present communication) to discuss the influence and the manner of spread of the practice of mummification in Europe. Reutter gives certain information in reference to this subject. It will suffice to say that there is no evidence to show that mummification was widely adopted until comparatively late times (New Empire and later) in the Mediterranean area, although certain effects of the Egyptian practice, such for example as "extended burial," spread abroad many centuries earlier, appearing in most regions during the Eneolithic phase.

The procedures revealed in the Canary Islands bear no trace of the influence of Negro Africa to which I have called attention (*supra*) in the Soudan, Uganda, the Congo and the Niger. The details of the technique suggests the method employed in the XXIst Dynasty; and other features seem to point to the conclusion that the practice must have reached the Canary Islands from the Western Mediterranean through the Straits of Gibraltar, not improbably through Phœnician channels.

[For a full critical discussion of all the literature relating to Egyptian influence in West Africa see Dahse, "Ein zweites Goldland Salomos," *Zeitsch. f. Ethn.*, 1911, p. 1. The mass of evidence collected in this memoir is entirely corroborative of the conclusions at which I have arrived from the study of mummification.]

With reference to Babylonia Langdon (**32**) states:—"Traces of embalming have not been found, but Herodotus says that the Babylonians preserved in honey. But a text has been discovered which mentions embalming with cedar oil (cited by Meissner, *Wiener Zeitsch. f. Kunde des Morgenlandes*, xii, 1898, p. 61). At any rate embalming is not characteristic of Babylonian burials and the custom may be due to Egyptian influence."

There can, I think, be no doubt whatever as to the Egyptian origin of these instances of embalming in Babylonia. The mere fact of its sporadic occurrence in a country of which it is not characteristic clearly points to this conclusion, which is confirmed by the emphasis laid upon the use of oil of cedar—a definite indication of the Egyptian practice. The reference of Herodotus to the use of honey in Babylonia is also of peculiar interest, for it provides us with a connecting link between the Mediterranean area and India and Burma.

The extensive use of honey for the preservation of the body among the Greeks, Romans, Jews, and possibly also the Egyptians, is indicated by the frequent references to the practice in the classics, which have been summarised, with numerous quotations, by Pettigrew (**56**, pp. 85-87).

The employment of honey suggests the spread of Egyptian influence to Babylonia *viâ* the Mediterranean and Syria, seeing that, so far as is known, such a method was used only on the Mediterranean littoral of Egypt, in Phœnicia and the Ægean.

Concerning the use of wax in the process of embalming, of which ancient Egyptian mummies, especially of the new Empire (**86**), afford numerous instances, Pettigrew (p. 87) remarks:—"The body of King Agesilaus was enveloped in wax and thus conveyed to Lacedæmon. This is confirmed by Cornelius Nepos, and also by Plutarch, who ascribe the adoption of wax to the want of honey for this purpose. Cicero reports the use of it by the Persians."

In his account of the methods employed by the Scythians (living north of Thrace) for mummifying their kings, Herodotus tells us that the body was coated with wax, the abdomen opened, cleaned out and then filled with pounded stems, with perfumes, aniseed and wild celery seed and then stitched up. The important bearing of the practices described in the Black Sea littoral upon Indian and Burmese customs (*vide infra*) I must reserve for discussion at some later time.

It will be seen in the subsequent account that honey was in use for embalming in modern times in Burma.

In an article on Persian burial customs (**32**, p. 505) Dr. Louis H. Gray says: "Unfortunately our sole information on this subject [Ancient Persian rites] must thus far be gleaned from the meagre statements of the classics. If we may judge from the tombs of the Achæmenians, their bodies were not exposed as Zoroastrianism dictated; but it is by no means impossible that they were coated with wax, or even, as Jackson[13] also suggests ("Persia, Past and Present," p. 235), 'perhaps embalmed

[13] Jackson refers the suggestion to Curzon's "Persia and the Persian Question," 1892, where I find (Vol. II., pp. 74, 79, 80, 146, 178 and 192) most conclusive evidence in proof of the fact that the body of Cyrus was mummified and all the Egyptian rites were observed (see especially Mr. Cecil Smith's note on p. 80). In Persia, under Darius (p. 182), the Egyptian methods of tomb-construction were closely copied, not only in their general plan, but in minute details of their decoration (see p. 178)—also the bas-relief of Cyrus wearing the Egyptian crown (p. 74). Cambyses even introduced Egyptian workmen to carry out such work (p. 192).

There are reasons for believing that India also was in turn influenced by this direct transmission of Egyptian practices to Persia, but only after (perhaps more than a century after) the Ethiopian modification of Egyptian embalming had been adopted there.

after the manner of the Egyptians.'"

In later times the Persians seem to have been influenced by the practices in vogue in Early Christian times in Egypt, before the coming of Islâm. Thus in Moll's History (**46**, p. 545), the statement is made in reference to the Moslem burial customs in Persia; "if it [the corpse] is to be buried a great way off, it is put into a wooden coffin filled up with salt, lime and perfumes to preserve it; for they embalm their dead bodies no otherwise in Persia, nor do they ever embowel them, as with us." That this is merely a degraded form of the Egyptian embalmer's practice is shown by the fact that it is identical with the method used by the Copts in Egypt until the seventh, or perhaps even as late as the ninth century A.D., and in their case we know that it is a development from, or degradation of, the ancient practice.

This method seems also to have spread to India: for Mr. Crooke tells me that even at the present day several of the ascetic orders bury their dead in salt.

In Moll's book the following curious statement also occurs, p. 474:—"*Mummy*, which is human flesh embalm'd that has lain in dry earth several ages, and become hard as horn, is frequently found in the sands of Chorassan, or the ancient Bactria, and some of the bodies are so little alter'd, 'tis said, that the features may be plainly distinguish'd."

In studying the easterly migration of the custom of mummification it is quite certain that the main stream of the wanderers who carried the knowledge to the east must have set out from the East African coast, because a whole series of modifications of the Egyptian method which were introduced in the Soudan and further south are also found in Indonesia, Polynesia and America. A curious feature of Egyptian embalming in the XIXth and especially the XXIst Dynasties (**78** and **86**) was the use of butter for packing the mummy. Among the Baganda, according to Roscoe, special importance came to be attached to this practice. Mr. Crooke has given me references from Indian literature (see especially *Journ. Anthr. Soc. Bombay*, Vol. I., 1886, p. 39) to bodies being "skilfully embalmed with heavenly drugs and *ghee*" [clarified butter].

The ancient Aryans used to disembowel the corpse and fill the cavity with *ghee* (Mitra, "Indo-Aryans," London, 1881, Vol. I., p. 135), as was done in the case of the mummy of the famous Pharaoh Meneptah (**86**).

The peculiarly Mediterranean modifications also spread east and it seems most likely that in this case the route from Syria down the Euphrates to the Persian Gulf was taken.

[Since this has been in print further investigation has elucidated with remarkable precision the ways and means of, as well as the impelling motives for, the great migration to the East. This calls for some modification of the foregoing (as well as many of the subsequent) paragraphs. It has been seen that the great wave of culture carried east and west from Egypt the distinctive method of embalming that came into full use somewhere about 900 B.C.; hence it is probable the eighth century B.C. witnessed the commencement of the series of expeditions, which probably extended over many centuries. It can be no mere chance that the period indicated coincides with the time when the Phœnicians were embarking upon maritime enterprises on a much greater and more daring scale than the world had known until then, in the Mediterranean and Atlantic, in the Red Sea and beyond. In the course of their trading expeditions to the Bab-el-Mandeb these Levantine mariners brought to that region a fuller knowledge of the customs and practices of Egypt and of the whole Phœnician world in the Mediterranean. It was probably in this way and not by the Euphrates route that the culture of the Levant reached the Persian Gulf and India.

The easterly migration of culture which set out from the region of the Bab-el-Mandeb conveyed not only the Ethiopian modifications of Egyptian practices, but also the Egyptian and Mediterranean contributions which the Phœnicians had brought to Ethiopia. On some future occasion I shall discuss the important part played by the Phœnicians in these expeditions to the Far East.]

It is unfortunate that practically nothing is known of the practice of mummification on the Southern coast of Arabia. Bent tells us that the Southern Arabians preserved their dead. Moreover, as the Egyptians obtained from Sabæa much of the materials used for embalming, it is not unlikely that the Arabs may also have learned the use of these preservatives.

In support of this suggestion I might refer to the evidence from Madagascar. It is well known that this island was colonised in ancient times by people from the neighbourhood of the Bab-el-Mandeb, probably Galla-people from the Somali coast as well as Sabæans from the Arabian coast, possibly ferried along the African shore by expert mariners from Oman and the Persian Gulf, either the Phœnicians themselves or their kinsmen. A more numerous element came from the distant Malay Archipelago. Either or both of these racial elements may have introduced the practice of mummification into Madagascar.

In his "History on Madagascar" (1838, Vol. I, p, 243) Ellis says there "was no regular embalming," but the "body was preserved for a time by the use of large quantities of gum benzoin, or other powdered aromatic gums." This method is strongly suggestive of South Arabian influence.

Hartland says "the Betsileo [and other Madagascar tribes] dry the corpse in the air, the fluids being assisted to escape" (**32**, p. 418).

Grandidier, however, gives us more precise information on this subject ("La Mort et les Funerailles à Madagascar," *L'Anthropologie*, T. 23, 1912, p. 329). According to him the Betsileo open the body of the dead and remove all the viscera, which they throw into a lake: among the Merina the entrails are removed only in the cases of their sovereigns or members of the royal family.

The practice of mummification amongst the Betsileo is of peculiar interest because the embalmed bodies are buried in stone tombs obviously inspired by Egyptian models. The subterranean megalithic burial chamber in association with an oblong *mastaba*-like superstructure at once recalls the distinctive features of the Egyptian tomb. But there is a curious feature suggestive of Babylonian influence, namely, the situation of the temple of offerings on the top of the *mastaba*. In some respects this type of grave recalls those found in the Bahrein Islands by Bent (**4**), which he compares with the Early Phœnician tombs at Arvad (**55**). There can be no question that the latter were copied from Theban tombs of the New Empire (*vide supra*).

This seems to point quite clearly to the fact that the Betsileo burial practices were inspired by Egyptian models, possibly modified by Southern Arabian influences.

In Hall's "Great Zimbabwe" (1905, pp. 94 and 95), it is stated that "the Baduma, who live in Gutu's country, and also the Barotse, still embalm, or, rather, dry the bodies of their chiefs, and also the dead of certain families, though generally the bodies are buried lengthways on their right side, facing the sun. The body is placed in the hut on a bier made of poles near a large fire, and continually turned until the body is dry. Then it is wrapped up in a blanket and hung from the roof" [as is done in the Doré Bay region in New Guinea].

There has been considerable controversy as to the origin of the vast stone monuments in this region. The writer from whom I have just quoted, with many others, believed the Zimbabwe ruins to be the work of Early Sabæan or Phœnician immigrants, who were attracted by the Rhodesian gold-fields. Randall-MacIver believed that he found Chinese and Persian relics (no earlier than the 14th or at earliest 13th century) under the foundations; and recklessly jumped to the conclusion that the local Negroes had conceived and built these vast monuments! The idea of any savage people, and especially Negroes, planning such structures and undertaking the enormous labour of their construction is surely too ludicrous to be considered seriously. Even if these monuments were built no earlier than five or six centuries ago, that does not invalidate the hypothesis that they were inspired by the models of some old civilization. Is it necessary to expound the whole theory of survivals to make this point clear? The whole of this memoir is concerned with the persistence in outlying corners of the world of strange practices whose inventors passed away twenty-eight centuries and more ago, and whose country has forgotten them and their works for more than a thousand years. [My friend, W. J. Perry, is collecting other evidence which proves quite definitely that the Zimbabwe culture was "heliolithic."]

In Moll's History (**46**) the following passage occurs in an account of the customs of Ceylon, p. 430, "when a person of condition dies his corps is laid out and wash'd, and being cover'd with a linnen-cloath, is carried out upon a bier to some high place and burnt: but if he was an officer who belong'd to the court, the corps is not burnt till the king gives orders for it, which is sometimes a great while after. In this case his friends hollow the body of a tree, and having bowell'd and embalm'd the corps, they put it in, filling the hollow up with pepper, and having made it as close as possible, they bury the corpse in some room of the house till the king orders it to be burnt."

"As for the poorer people, they usually wrap them up in mats and bury them."

This traveller's tale would not call for serious attention if it were not confirmed by modern accounts of an analogous practice in Burma and the neighbourhood.

In his "Himalayan Journal" Sir Joseph Hooker described how the Khasias temporarily embalm their dead in honey before cremating them.

Pettigrew (**56**, p. 245) quotes Captain Coke's account of the embalming of a Burman priest. The body, as witnessed by him, was lying exposed to public view upon a stage constructed of bamboos. This is the bier which is so invariably associated with mummification.

"The entrails of the deceased (who had been dead upwards of a month) had been taken out a few hours after death by means of an incision in the stomach, and the vacuum being filled with honey and spices the opening was sewed up. The whole body was then covered over with a slight coating of resinous substance called *dhamma*, and wax, to preserve it from the air, after which it was richly overlaid with gold leaf, thus giving the body the appearance of one of the finely moulded images so common in the temples of the worshippers of Boodh."

Then it was cremated.

This is a curious instance of the blending of the custom of mummification with the later practice of cremation, which was inspired by entirely different ideals. Throughout the whole area in which Egyptian methods of embalming were adopted there are found numerous instances of such syncretism with a variety of burial customs.

"Another method which I have known to be practised, but not as common as the one above detailed, of embalming bodies in the Burman country, is by forcing two hollow bamboos through the soles of the feet, up the legs and into the body of the deceased; then by dint of pressing and squeezing the fluid is carried off through the bamboos into the ground."

This practice is an important link between the Egyptian and the Indonesian methods.

In his article on Thibetan burial customs (**32**, p. 511), Waddell informs us that preservation of the entire body by embalming seems to be restricted to the sovereign Grand Lamas of Lhāsa and Tāshilhumpo. "The body is embalmed by salting, and, clad in the robes of the deceased and surrounded by his personal implements of worship, is placed, in the attitude of a seated Buddha, within a gilded copper sarcophagus in one of the rooms of the palace: it is then worshipped as a divinity."

There are many points of interest in this practice, which, considered in conjunction with the methods practised in Burma, Ceylon and Persia just mentioned, clearly indicate not only the sources and the routes taken by this knowledge of embalming in its spread from Egypt, but also how the burial rites of a variety of peoples can become intimately blended and intermingled one with another.

In Captain T. H. Lewins' book on "The Wild Tribes of South-Eastern India" (London, 1870, p. 274) I find the following statement:—"Among the Dhun and Khorn clans the body is placed in a coffin made of a hollow tree trunk, with holes in the bottom. This is placed on a lofty platform and left to dry in the sun. The dried body is afterwards rammed into an earthern vase and buried; the head is cut off and preserved. Another clan sheathe their dead in pith; the corpse is then placed on a platform, under which a slow fire is kept up until the body is dried. The corpse is then kept for six months ... it is then buried. The Howlong clan hang the body up to the house-beams for seven days, during which time the dead man's wife has to sit underneath spinning."

These interesting records are of considerable value in establishing connexions between East Africa and regions further east, which will be discussed in the following pages.

[In my search for information concerning the practice of embalming in India, where by inference I was convinced it must have had some vogue in ancient times, I completely overlooked the important memoir by Mr. W. Crooke on "Primitive Rites of Disposal of the Dead, with Special Reference to India" (*Journ. Anthrop. Inst.*, Vol. XXIX, 1899, p. 272). Since the rest of this article has been in print Mr. Crooke has kindly called my attention to his memoir and given me a lot of other valuable information. Fortunately all this evidence supports and substantiates the opinions I had previously arrived at inductively. For it provides a complete series of connecting links between the western and eastern portions of the chain I am reconstructing. It is too bulky to insert here and too important merely to summarise, so that I must postpone fuller discussion of this Indian evidence until some future time.]

If it is admitted that the custom of mummification as it is practised, for example, in the islands of the Torres Straits was derived from Egypt, however remotely and indirectly, it is clear that, as the technique includes a number of curious features which were not introduced in Egypt before the XVIIIth, XXth and XXIst Dynasties (respectively in the case of different procedures), the migration of people carrying the methods east could not have left Egypt before the time of the XXIst Dynasty, say 900 B.C. as the earliest possible date. At this time Egypt was in very close relationship with the Soudan and Western Asia; and it is obvious that the Egyptian practices may have reached the Persian Gulf by three routes:— (1) *viâ* the Soudan, the head-waters of the Nile and the Somali Coast, (2) by the Red Sea route, and (3) from the Phœnician Coast down the Euphrates. No doubt all three routes served as avenues for communication and for the transmission of cultural influences; and it is not essential for our immediate purposes to enquire which channel served to transmit each element of Egyptian culture that made its influence felt in the neighbourhood of the Persian Gulf at this period. For it was a period of active maritime enterprise, especially on the part of the Phœnicians, both in the Mediterranean and the Southern Seas, and a time when the fluctuating political fortunes of Egypt, Western Asia and the Soudan produced a more intimate intermingling of the peoples, so that they mutually influenced one another most profoundly.

It is important to remember that many of the features of the embalmer's art as it is practiced in the far East are modifications of the Egyptian method which were first introduced in the region of the Upper Nile, so that the East African Coast must have been the point of departure for such methods. Other features, not only of the method of embalming, but also of the associated megalithic architecture, were equally distinctive of the Phœnician region and may have been transmitted by the Euphrates.[14] Other features again were distinctively Babylonian. Of the

[14] See, however, p. 69. At some future time I shall explain what an important link is provided by the ancient culture of the Black Sea littoral between Egypt and the civilizations

former, the African influence, I might refer to the use of the frame-like support for the mummy, the custom of removing the head some months after burial, and the sacrifice of wives and servants. As to the Phœnician and Babylonian influences, the use of honey might be cited, and the emphasis laid upon "cedar" wood and "cedar" oil in mummification; and the Phœnician adaptation of the New Empire type of Theban tomb seen at Arvad and the analogous sepulchres found in the Bahrein Islands (4) The Betsileo tombs in Madagascar probably represent the same type transferred *viâ* Sabæa down the East African coast.

As to the means by which the customs of the dwellers around the Persian Gulf were communicated to the peoples of India and Ceylon there is a considerable mass of evidence. The fact that mummification, the building of megalithic monuments of the recognised Mediterranean types, sun- and serpent-worship and all the other impedimenta of the "heliolithic" culture made their appearance in India in pre-Aryan times affords positive evidence of the reality of the intercourse. I have already referred to the adoption in India of the curiously eccentric method of steering river-boats found in Middle Kingdom Egyptian tombs; and the custom of representing eyes on the prow of the boat are further illustrations of the spread of distinctive practices. According to Rhys Davids (**14**, p. 116) "it may now be accepted as a working hypothesis that sea-going merchants [mostly Dravidians, not Aryans], availing themselves of the monsoons, were in the habit, at the beginning of the seventh (and perhaps at the end of the eighth) century B.C., of trading from ports on the South-West of India to Babylon, then a great mercantile emporium." He adduces evidence which clearly demonstrates that the written scripts of India, Ceylon and Burma were in this way derived from "the pre-Semitic race now called Akkadians." "It seems almost impossible to avoid the conclusion that [the] curious buildings [at Anurādhapura in Ceylon] were not entirely without connection with the seven-storied Ziggarats which were so striking a feature among the buildings of Chaldæa.... it would seem that in this case also the Indians were borrowers of an idea" (p. 70). The more precise and definite influence of Babylonian models further east removes any doubt as to the part it played. Crooke speaks of the Southern Dravidians as a maritime people, who placed in their burial mounds "bronze articles which were probably imported in the course of trade with Babylonia" (**12**, p. 29). "They were probably the builders of the remarkable series of rude stone monuments which crown the hills in the Nilgiri range and the plateau of the Deccan" (p. 28). The most ancient stone monuments in Southern India contain objects which go to prove that they were built at the earliest just before the introduction of iron-working. Thus, if the knowledge of iron-working came from Europe, these monuments could not have been built much before 800 B.C. As a matter of fact it is known that many of them cannot be older than 600 B.C. (Crooke, **13**, p. 129). All of these facts agree in supporting the view that the influence of Egypt, which, so far as the matters under consideration are concerned, came into operation not earlier than the eighth century B.C., spread to India partly *viâ* Babylonia and partly by way of East Africa, somewhere between the close of the eighth and the commencement of the sixth century B.C.

---

of the Western Mediterranean on the one hand and India on the other.

The monuments to which I have just been referring were not, in my opinion, directly inspired by Egypt, but indirectly. The North Syrian and the adjoining territories adopted the Egyptian burial customs at an earlier period and the finished type of holed dolmen was probably developed and survived in that region long after its Egyptian prototype had become a thing of the past. The real types that have come down to our times are found in the Caucasus, between the Black Sea and the Caspian. The Indian dolmens were certainly imitations of these models. But in respect of other buildings the Indians directly adopted Babylonian and Egyptian types. I have already referred to the former. Many of the Dravidian temples are so precisely modelled on the plan of the Theban temples of the New Empire that to question the source of the inspiration of the former is impossible.

"Fergusson first called attention to the striking similarity in general arrangement and conception between the great South Indian temples and those of ancient Egypt.... The gopurams or gate-towers, which in the later more ornate examples are decorated from the base to the summit with sculptures of the Hindu Pantheon, increase in size with the size of the walled quadrangles, the outer ones becoming imposing landmarks, which are visible for miles around, and are strikingly similar to the pylons of Egyptian temples" (Thurston, **101**, pp. 158 and 161). Thus in the matter of its early buildings India has clearly been influenced by Egypt, Phœnicia and Chaldea; and this great cultural wave impinged upon the Indian peninsula not before the close of the eighth century B.C.

It is important also to remember that it reached India just (perhaps not more than a century) before another wave of a very different culture poured down from the north, and introduced, among other things, the practice of cremation.

For our immediate purpose this is unfortunate, because that practice is inspired by ideas utterly opposed to those underlying the custom of embalming, and naturally destroyed most, though by no means all, traces of the latter. That the practice of embalming did actually reach India from the west is known not merely because evidence of unmistakably Egyptian technique is found further east, but also because in India and Ceylon there are definite traces of the custom, to which reference has already been made in the foregoing pages. Cases from Persia, Ceylon, India, Burma and Thibet were cited in proof of the survival of elements of the embalming process or ritual, even when the Brahmanical and Buddhist burial practices had been adopted.

From the foregoing account there can be no doubt that the people of India did at one time practice mummification, at any rate in the case of their chiefs. They also acquired a knowledge of the arts and crafts, as the result of the influence exerted by the rich stream of culture which brought the attainments of the great western civilizations to India before the Ayran immigration. The bringers of this new culture mingled their blood with the aboriginal pre-Dravidian population and the result was the Dravidians. It is not at all improbable that the resultant Dravidian civilization had reached a higher plane than that of the Aryas, who entered the country after them.

In Oldham's interesting and suggestive brochure (**51**, pp. 53-55), which, in spite of Crooke's drastic criticism, seems to me to be a valuable contribution to a knowledge of the questions under discussion, the following passages occur:—

"The Asuras, Dasyus, or Nagas, with whom the Aryas came into contact, on approaching the borders of India, were no savage aboriginal tribes, but a civilized people who had cities and castles. Some of these are said in the Veda to have been built of stone.

"It would seem, indeed, as if the Asuras had reached a higher degree of civilization than their Aryan rivals. Some of their cities were places of considerable importance. And, in addition to this, wealth and luxury, the use of magic, superior architectural skill, and ability to restore the dead to life, were ascribed to the Asuras by Brahmanical writers."

The "ability to restore the dead to life" is probably a reference to the Egyptian ritual of "the opening of the mouth," which of course is an integral part of the funerary procedure incidental to the practice of mummification.

"The Nagas occupy a very prominent position in connection with Indian astronomy, and this is not likely to have been assigned to them, by their Brahmanical rivals, without good reason. Probably this and other branches of science were brought, by the Asuras, from their ancient home in the countries between the Kaspian and the Persian Gulf.

"The close relationship between the Indian and the Chaldean astronomical systems has been frequently noticed.

"The sun-worship of the Asuras; their holding sacred the Naga or hooded serpent, sometimes represented with many heads; their deification of kings and ancestors; their veneration of the cedar; their religious dances; their sacrificial rights; their communication with the deities through the medium of inspired prophets; their occasional tendency towards democratic institutions; their use of tribal emblems or totems—and many of their social customs; seem to connect them with that very early civilization—Turanian or otherwise—which we find amongst so many of the peoples of extreme antiquity. They had, in fact, much in common with the early inhabitants of Babylonia; and, perhaps, even more with those of Elam and the neighbouring countries.

"We shall see later that the Asuras and the Dravidians were, apparently, the same people."

"Not only were the Asuras or Nagas a civilized people, but they were a maritime power. Holding both banks of the great river Indus, they must have had access to the sea from a very early period. Their kinship, too, with the serpent-worshipping people of ancient Media, and the neighbouring countries, which has already been referred to, must have led to a very early development of trade with the Persian Gulf.

"The Asuras were actively engaged in 'The Churning of the Ocean' (*Mahabharata, Adi, Astika*, p. xviii.), which is but an allegorical description of sea-borne commerce in its early days" (*op. cit.*, p. 58).

"In the *Mahabharata*, the ocean is described as the habitation of the Nagas and the residence of the Asuras; it is also said to be the refuge of the defeated Asuras (*Mahabharata, Adi, Astika*, p. xxii.). This was no doubt because marauding bands of this people retreated to their ships after an unsuccessful raid. Thus we find that on the death of Vrita, his followers took refuge in the sea (*Mahabharata, Vana, Tirtha-yatra*, p. ciii.). So also did the Asura Panchajana, who lived in Patala, when he was pursued by Krishna (*Vishnu Parana*, v., xxi., 526). And so did the Danavas when defeated by the Devas at the churning of the ocean (*Mahabharata, Adi, Astika*, p. xix.)."

"An ancient legend, given in the *Mahabharata*, relates how Kadru, mother of the serpents, compelled Garuda to convey her sons across the sea into a beautiful country in a distant region, which was inhabited by Nagas. After encountering a violent storm and great heat, the sons of Karur were landed in the country of Ramaniaka, on the Malabar coast."

"This territory had been occupied previously by a fierce Asura named Lavana (*Mahabharata, Adi, Astika*, p. xxvii.). So there had been a still earlier colonization by the same race."

"Naga chiefs are frequently mentioned as ruling countries in or under the sea" (p. 61).

"The civilization of Burmah, and other Indo-Chinese countries, is ascribed by legend and by the native historians to invaders from India. And these are connected with the Naga People of Magadha, and of the north and west of India. The ancient navigators, too, who carried the Brahmanical and Buddhist religions, the worship of the Naga, and the Sanscrit or Pali language to Java, Sumatra, and even to distant Celebes, were Indian people. And they were, doubtless, descendants of those Asura dwellers in the ocean, which are mentioned in the *Mahabharata*, and have already been referred to" (p. 166).

"Another proof of the ancient connection of these islands with India is that the Javan era is the Saka-kala, which is so well known, and is still in use in parts of Western India and in the Himalaya. According to a Javan tradition an expedition from India, led by a son of the king of Kujrat (Gujrat), arrived on the west coast of the island about A.D. 603. A settlement was founded, and the town of Mendan Kamalan was built. Other Hindus followed, and a great trade was established with the ports of India and other countries (Raffles, Hist. Java, ii., 83). There is however no reason to suppose that this was the first arrival of Indian voyagers in the Archipelago.

"Traditions still remain in Western India of expeditions to Java. A Guzerati proverb runs thus: 'He who goes to Java never comes back; but if he does return, his descendants, for seven generations, live at ease' (*Bombay Gazetter*, i., 402). The bards in Marwar have a legend that Bhoj raja, the great puar chief of Ujaini, in anger drove away his son Chandrabhan, who sailed to Java (*Ib.*, i., 448).

"Evidence brought forward by Mr. Kennedy (*J. R. A. S.*, April, 1898) shows that a great sea-borne trade was carried on from Indian ports by Dravidian merchants as early as the seventh century B.C. The beginnings of Dravidian navigation, however, were probably much earlier than this.

"We have seen that the sea-borne commerce of the Solar or Naga tribes of Western India had become important at a very early period. Of this the legend of 'the churning of the ocean' already referred to is an allegorical description, but we have no detailed account of ocean voyages until a much later period. Sakya Buddha himself, however, refers to such voyages. He says: 'Long ago ocean going merchants were wont to plunge forth upon the sea, taking with them a shore-sighting bird. When the ship was out of sight of land they would set the shore-sighting bird free. And it would go to the east and to the south and to the west and to the north and to the intermediate points and rise aloft. If on the horizon it caught sight of land, thither it would go. But if not then it would come back to the ship again' (Rhys Davids, *J. R. A. S.*, April, 1899, 432).

"It will be observed that this mode of finding the position of the ship at sea, which recalls the sending out of the birds from the Ark, is said to have been the custom 'long ago.' It would seem therefore, that in the fifth century B.C. other and probably more scientific methods were in use. It would also appear that the navigation of the ocean was even then an ancient institution.

"In the time of the Chinese Buddhist pilgrim Fah Hian (about 406 A.D.) there was a regular and evidently old-established trade between India and China and with the islands of the Archipelago.

"Fah Hian sailed from Tamalitti, or Tamralipti, at the mouth of the Ganges, in a great merchant ship, and in fourteen days reached Ceylon (Fo-Kwo-ki, Beal., I, lxxi, lxxii.). From thence he sailed in a great ship which carried about two hundred men, and which was navigated by observing the sun, moon and stars. In this ship Fah Hian reached Ye-po-ti (probably Java) in which country heretics and Brahmans flourished, but the law of Buddha was not much known (*Ib.*, I, lxxx.). Here the pilgrim embarked for China on board another ship carrying two hundred men, amongst whom were Brahmans. These proposed to treat the sramana as Jonah was treated, and for the same reason, but some of those on board took his part. At length when their provisions were nearly exhausted, they reached China (*Ib.*, I, lxxxi., lxxxii.). All these ships appear to have been Indian and not Chinese.

"Fah Hian mentions that pirates were numerous in those seas (*Ib.*, I, lxxx.), which shows that the commerce must have been considerable" (p. 171).

"It seems in the highest degree improbable that this close connection between the Sun and the serpent could have originated, independently, in countries so far apart as China and the West of Africa, or India and Peru. And it seems scarcely possible that, in addition to this, the same forms of worship of these deities, and the same ritual, could have arisen, spontaneously, amongst each of these far distant peoples. The alternative appears to be that the combined worship of the Sun and serpent-gods must have spread from a common centre, by the migration of, or communication with, the people who claimed Solar descent.

"So universally was the Naga held sacred, that it would seem to have been the earliest totem of the people who claimed descent from the Sun-god" (p. 183).

I have quoted so extensively from Oldham's fascinating work because the conclusions at which he arrived from a study of the ancient literature of India is confirmed by evidence derived from utterly different sources, not only from India itself but also from other countries. For, scattered throughout the length and breadth of India, are to be found thousands of indications (in traditions, beliefs, customs, social organisation and material relics) that the complete "heliolithic" culture had reached India not later than the beginning of the seventh century B.C.

Moreover the evidence which I have culled from Oldham bears out the conclusions my own investigations lead up to, namely, that the "heliolithic" culture spread from India to Malaysia soon after it reached India itself. It is surely something more than a mere coincidence that the period of the greatest maritime exploits of the Phœnicians, in the course of which, according to many authorities, they reached India or even further east, should coincide with that of the great pre-Aryan maritime race of India, whose great expeditions, as the above quotations indicate, were primarily for purposes of commerce between the Persian Gulf and the West Coast of India. There is gradually accumulating a considerable mass of evidence to suggest that, if the Asuras were not themselves Phœnicians, they acquired their maritime skill from these famous sailors and traders. The same hardy mariners who brought the new knowledge and practices from the Persian Gulf to India and Ceylon also carried it further, to Burma and Indonesia.

That this is so is clearly shown by the fact that these customs spread to Indonesia and the Pacific *before* cremation was introduced; and it has been indicated above that the introduction of the practice of cremation into India may have taken place within a century of the arrival of the "heliolithic" civilization there. Hence it is obvious that the latter must have spread to the far east soon after it reached India; and the completeness of the transmission of the distinctive culture-complex can be explained only by supposing that the same people who brought it to India also carried it further east.

All the other evidence at our disposal is in full harmony with this view. The advancing wave of western culture swept past India into Indonesia, carrying into the isles of the Pacific and on to the American littoral the products of the older civilizations at first almost, but not altogether, untainted by Indian influence; but for centuries afterwards, as this same ferment gradually leavened the vast bulk of India, the stream of western culture continued to percolate eastwards and carried with it in succession the influence of the Brahmanical, Buddhist and, within in a more restricted area, Mahometan cults.

It is an interesting confirmation of the general accuracy of the scheme that has now been sketched out that the dates at which the influence of Egypt began to be exerted in the east, that to which Rhys Davids assigns the definite influencing of India by Babylonia, that at which India influenced Malaysia, and finally that assigned by students of the Polynesian problem to the inauguration of the great Indonesian migration into the Pacific (**60** and **98**), all fit into one consecutive series, though each was determined from different kinds of evidence and independently of the rest.

It is not my intention to discuss the evidence for the coming of the "heliolithic" culture to Indonesia, for the complex problems of this region have been analysed and interpreted in a masterly fashion by W. J. Perry in a book which is shortly to be published. The form which my present communication has assumed is largely the outcome of the reading of Perry's manuscript and of discussions with him of the new lines of investigation which it suggested; and I am satisfied to leave this region for him to elucidate in detail. It will suffice to say here that the traditions of the inhabitants of the various islands of Malaysia, no less than their heterogeneous customs and beliefs, provided him with very precise evidence in demonstration of the complex constitution of the "heliolithic" culture, and of the fact that it was brought to the islands by an immigration from the west.

There is less need for me to analyse the vast literature relating to the burial practices in the islands of the Malay Archipelago since this useful service has already been accomplished by Hertz (**33**). Although I dissent from the main contention in his interpretation of the facts, his accurate record is none the less valuable on that account—perhaps indeed it is more useful, as it certainly cannot be accused of bias in favour of the views I am expounding.

A great variety of burial customs, in most respects closely analogous to the practices of the Naga tribes of India, is found in Indonesia;—exposing the dead on trees or platforms, burial in hollow trees, smoking and other methods of preservation, temporary burial, and cremation.

Apart from the definite evidence of preservation of the dead found in scattered islands from one end of the Archipelago to the other, there are much more generally diffused practices which are unquestionably derived from the former custom of mummification.

In the account of mummification as practised in the more savage African tribes, it was seen that the practice was restricted in most cases to the bodies of kings; and even then the failure to preserve the body in a permanent manner compelled these peoples to modify the Egyptian methods. Realising that the corpse, even when preserved as efficiently as they were able to perform the work of embalming, would undergo a process of disintegration within a few months, it became the practice to rescue the skull, to which special importance was attached (for the definite reasons explained by the early Egyptian evidence).

In his survey Hertz (**33**, p. 66) calls attention to the widespread custom of temporary burial throughout Indonesia, but, instead of recognising that such procedures have come into vogue as a degradation of the full rites incidental to mummification, he regards it as part of a widespread "notion que les derniers rites funéraires ne peuvent pas être célébrés de suite après la mort, mais seulement à l'expiration d'une période plus on moins longue" (p. 66); and regards mummification simply as a specialised form of this rite which is almost universal (p. 67):—"il paraît légitime de considérer la momification comme un cas particulier et dérivé de la sépulture provisoire." (p. 69). This is a remarkable inversion of the true explanation. For the enormous mass of evidence which is now available makes it quite certain that the practice of temporary burial was adopted only when failure (or the risk of failure) to preserve the body compelled less cultured people to desist from the complete process.

I am in full agreement with Hertz when he says:—"L'homologie entre la préservation artificielle du cadavre et la simple exposition temporaire paraîtra moins difficile à admettre si l'on tient compte du fait qui sera mis en lumière plus bas: les ossements secs, résidu de la décomposition, constituent pour le mort un corps incorruptible, absolument comme la momie." (p. 69). But does not this entirely bear out my contention? It is quite inconceivable that the practice of mummification could have been derived from the custom of preparing the skeleton; but the reverse is quite a natural transition, for even in the hands of skilled embalmers (see especially **39**), not to mention untutored savage peoples, the measures taken for preserving the body may fail and the skeleton alone may be spared. If this contention be conceded, the demonstration given by Hertz of the remarkable geographical distribution of customs of temporary burial affords a most valuable confirmation of the general scheme of the present communication. "Au point de vue où, nous sommes placés, il y a homologie rigoureuse entre l'exposition du cadavre sur les branches d'un arbre, telle que la pratiquent les tribus du centre de l'Australie, ou à l'intèrieur de la maison des vivants, comme cela se rencontre chez certains Papous et chez quelques peuples Bantous, ou sur une plateforme élevée à dessein, ainsi que le font en général les Polynésiens et de nombreuses tribus indiennes de l'Amérique du Nord, ou enfin l'enterrement provisoire, observé en particulier par la plupart des Indiens de l'Amérique du Sud" (p. 67). There can be no doubt whatever of the justice of this "homology," for in every one of the areas mentioned these customs exist side by side with the practice of mummification; and in many cases there is definite evidence to show that the other methods of treatment have been derived from it by a process of degradation. In his excellent bibliography, and especially the illuminating footnotes, Hertz gives a number of references to the practice of desiccation by smoking or simple forms of embalming, which had escaped me in my search for information on these matters. He refers especially to further instances of such practices in Australia, New Guinea, various parts of West Africa, Madagascar and America (p. 68).

An interesting reference in the same note (p. 68, footnote 5) is to the practice of simple embalming among the Ainos of Sakhalin (Preuss, *Begräbnisarten der Amerikaner*, p. 190). This seems to supply an important link between the Eastern Asiatic littoral and the Aleutian Islands, where mummification is practised. In Saghalien, according to St. John ("The Ainos," *Journ. Anthropol. Inst.*, Vol. II., 1873, p. 253), "when the chief of a tribe or village died, his body was laid out on a table close to the door of his hut; his entrails were then removed, and daily for twelve months his wife and daughters wash him thoroughly. He is allowed ... to dry in the sun."

In a recent article on the customs of the people of Laos (G. Maupetit, "Moeurs laotiennes," *Bull. et Mem. de la Soc. d' Anthropol. de Paris*, 1913), an account is given of the practice of mummification in this far south-eastern corner of the Asiatic mainland. Cremation is the regular means adopted for disposal of the dead: but it is also "the Laotian's ideal to be able to preserve the corpse in his house, for as long a time as possible, before incinerating it: in the same way the Siamese and Chinese keep their dead in the house for several months, often for several years" (p. 549).

According to Maupetit the method of preservation is a most remarkable one.

They pour from 75 to 300 grammes of mercury into the mouth! "It passes along the alimentary canal and suffices to produce mummification, the rapid desiccation of the organic tissues." Then the body was stretched upon a thick bed of melted wax, wood ashes, cloth and cushions.

The great stream of "heliolithic" culture exerted a profound influence upon and played a large part in shaping the peculiar civilizations of China, Corea, and Japan. As the practice of embalming does not play an obtrusive part[15] in this influence, I do not propose (in the present communication) to enter upon the discussion of these matters, except to note in passing that the influence exerted by the "heliolithic" culture upon the Pacific coast of America may have been exerted partly by the East Asiatic-Aleutian route (see *Map II.*).

The disgusting practice of collecting the fluids which drip from the putrefying corpse and mixing them with the food for the living occurs in Indonesia, in New Guinea and the neighbouring islands, in Melanesia, Polynesia and in Madagascar (for the bibliographical references see Hertz, p. 83, footnote 3).

The Indonesian methods of preserving the dead are found in Seram (W. J. Perry), and the report recently published by Lorenz[16] (**43**, p. 22) records a similar practice in the neighbourhood of Doré Bay in North-West New Guinea. The corpse was tied to the rafter of the dwelling-house; and the practice of mixing the juices of decomposition with the food is in vogue also. The accounts given by D'Albertis (**1**) and other travellers show that analogous customs are found at other places in New Guinea. There can be no doubt that the practice spread along the north coast of the island and then around its eastern extremity to reach the islands of the Torres Straits, where the practice is seen in its fully developed form, as Flower (**19**), Haddon and Myers (**25**), and Hamlyn-Harris (**27**) have described.

As I have already referred to Papuan mummies earlier in this communication and at some future time intend to devote a special memoir to the full discussion of the methods of the Torres Straits embalmers, I shall not go into the matter in detail here. I should like, however, to call special attention to the admirable account given by Haddon and Myers (**25**) of the associated funeral rites.

In his memoir Flower described two interesting mummies, then in the Museum of the Royal College of Surgeons in London, one "brought in 1872 from Darnley Island in Torres Strait by Mr. Charles Lemaistre, Captain of the French barque 'Victorine,' and the other, an Australian mummy, obtained in 1845 near Adelaide, by Sir George Grey." By a curious and utterly incomprehensible act of vandalism these extremely rare and priceless ethnological specimens were deliberately destroyed by Sir William Flower, who naively explains his extraordinary action by the statement "as the skeleton will form a more instructive specimen when the dried and decaying integuments are removed I have had it cleaned" (p. 393)! He treated in the same manner the second mummy, the only example of its

[15] Reuter (**63**) quotes the statement from Tschirch that Neuhof has described the embalming of bodies in Asia. In Borneo camphor, areca nut and the wood of aloes and musk are used; and in China camphor and sandalwood.

[16] For this and certain other references I have to thank my colleague Professor S. J. Hickson, F.R.S. So far I have been unable to consult the full reports of Lorenz's expedition.

kind, so far as I am aware, in this country! His photographs show that these two specimens, so far from being "decaying," were in a remarkably good state of preservation at the time he doomed them to destruction.

Captain Lemaistre found the Torres Strait mummy "in its grave, which consisted of a high straw and bamboo hut of round form: it was not lying down, but standing up on the stretcher" (**19**, p. 389). This is a close parallel to the African customs—mummification, burial in a house of round form, and fixing the corpse to a rough form of funeral bier, which is stood up in the house.

The skin was painted red, the scalp black. "The sockets of the eyes were filled with a dark brown substance, apparently a vegetable gum.... In this was imbedded a narrow oval piece of mother of pearl, pointed at each end, in the centre of the anterior surface of which is fixed a round mass of the same resinous substance, representing the pupil of the eye" (p. 301).

"Both nostrils had been distended."

"In the right flank was a longitudinal incision, 3½ inches in length, extending between the last rib and the crest of the ilium. This had been very neatly closed by what is called in surgery the interrupted suture.... The whole of the pelvic, abdominal and thoracic viscera had been removed, and their place was occupied by four pieces of very soft wood.... Except the wound in the flank, there was no other opening or injury to the skin" (p. 391).

"Heads and bodies prepared in a similar way" are found in many museums, and afford an interesting illustration of the old Egyptian practice of paying special attention to the head. This is all the more instructive in view of the fact that it was common in certain regions, especially Mallicolo in the New Hebrides, to restore the features by means of clay and resinous paste, usually making use of the skull as a basis, but occasionally modelling the whole body,[17] the model including parts of the deceased's skeleton (see Henry Balfour's article, "Memorial Heads in the Pitt Rivers Museum," *Man*, Vol. I., 1901, p. 65). These modelling-practices and especially the fact that they usually deal with the head (or even face) only afford an interesting confirmation of the Egyptian origin of these customs (*vide supra*, etc., **40**).

In the 6th volume of the reports of the Cambridge Anthropological Expedition to Torres Straits, C. S. Myers and Haddon (**25**, pp. 129 and 135) give a detailed account of the funeral ceremonies from which I quote certain points. "As soon as death had occurred the women of the village started wailing. The corpse was placed on the ground on a mat in front of the house; the arms were placed close to the side; the great toes were tied together by a string; the hair of the head and face was cut off and thrown away; the length of the nose was then measured with a piece of wax, which was preserved by a female relative for subsequent use in making a wax mask for the prepared skull. The dead man's bow and arrow and his stone-headed club were laid beside him" (p. 129). The Egyptian analogies in all of these procedures is quite obvious.

---

[17] A curious feature of these models is the representation of faces on the shoulders. Similar practices have been recorded in America (Bancroft, **3**).

"Five men wearing masks performed a series of manœuvres ending up with flexion of the arms and a bending of the head. This movement was said to indicate the rising and setting of the sun and to be symbolic of the life and death of man.

"Mourners then took the body and placed it upon a wooden framework, which stood upon four wooden supports at a little distance from the house of the deceased. The relatives then took large yams and placed them beside the body on the framework; they also hung large bunches of bananas upon the bamboos around. This was regarded as nourishment for the ghost, which was supposed to eat it at night-time (p. 135).

"In two or three days when the skin of the body had become loose the framework was taken up to the reef in a small canoe; the epidermis was then rubbed off and by means of a sharp shell a small incision was made in the side of the abdomen (in the right side, at least, in the case of women), whence the viscera were extracted.

"The perineum was incised in the males."

From a study of all the literature regarding this custom, as well as the actual specimens now in Sydney and Brisbane, it is clear that the incision may be made either in the left or right flank or in the perineum, and that sex does not determine the site.

"The abdominal cavity was then filled up with pieces of Nipa palm; the viscera were thrown into the sea and the incision closed by means of fine fish line. An arrow was used to remove the brain, partly by way of the foramen magnum and partly through a small slit which was made in the back of the neck. The 'strong skin' of the brain (the dura mater) was first cut and then the 'soft skin' was pulled out.

"The body was then brought back to the island and was placed in a sitting position upon a stone; the entire body was then painted with a mixture of red earth and sea water. The head, body and limbs were then lashed to the framework with string and a small stick was affixed to the lower jaw to keep it from drooping. The framework, with its burden, was fastened vertically to two posts set up in the rear of the house, and it was protected from public view by a screen of coconut leaves. The body was then gently rubbed down and holes were made with the point of an arrow so that the juices might escape. A fire was always kept alight beneath the body, 'by-n-by meat swell up' (p. 136).

"D'Albertis (1) saw in Darnley Island the mummy of a man, who had been dead over a year, standing in the middle of the widow's house attached to a kind of upright ladder of poles. They tint him from time to time with red chalk (ochre) and keep his skin soft by anointing it with coconut oil" (p. 137).

In the Berlin Museum für Volkerkunde there are mummies of two children, photographs of which, obtained from Professor von Luschan, are reproduced by Dr. Haddon. They were given to Dr. Bastian by the Rev. James Chamlers in 1880, having been obtained at Stephen's Island. One of them is a small girl a few days old. The body is painted red all over, except the scalp and eyebrows, which are blackened. The other one was a small girl two or three years of age treated in a similar way; the incision for embalming is on the *left* side and has been sewn up.

"In 1845 Jukes saw on the lap of a woman of Darnley Island the body of a child a few months old which seemed to have been dead for some time. It was stretched on a framework of sticks and smeared over with a thick red pigment, which dressing she was engaged in renewing. ("Voyage of the 'Fly,'" Vol. I., 1847, p. 246)" (p. 138).

"Macgillivray ("Voyage of the 'Rattlesnake,'" Vol. II., 1852, p. 48) also refers to a mummy of a child in Darnley Island. Sketches of the two Miriam mummies in the Brisbane Museum will be found on Plate 94 of Edge Partington and Heape's Ethnographical Album of the Pacific Islands, third series. [Compare also Plate 2, Figure 4, in Brockett's "Voyage to Torres Straits," Sydney, 1836]" (p. 137).

"On about the tenth day after death, when the hands and feet have become partially dried, the relatives, using a bamboo knife, remove the skin of the palms and soles, together with the nails, and then cut out the tongue, which is put into a bamboo clamp so that it may be kept straight while drying. These were presented to the widow, who henceforth wore them" (p. 138).

A great deal of further information in regard to this practice is given by Haddon and Myers in their important monograph. Among other things they call attention once more to the custom of preserving the skull in the Torres Straits Islands where mummification is practised. The use of masks and ceremonial dances to assist the performers so as the more realistically to play the part of the deceased is welcome confirmation of the conclusion drawn from geographical distribution that such practices were intimately related to mummification and form part of the ritual genetically linked to it.

Dr. Hamlyn-Harris, the Director of the Queensland Museum, gives an account (**27**) of the two mummies from the Torres Straits, which are now in Brisbane; and he adds further interesting information which he obtained from Mr. J. S. Bruce, of Murray Island, who was also one of Dr. Haddon's informants. During my recent visit to Australia Dr. Hamlyn-Harris very kindly gave me every facility for examining these two mummies (as well as the Australian mummies in the Queensland Museum); and I also examined another specimen in the Macleay Museum of the University of Sydney. I am preparing a full report on all of these interesting specimens.

From the Torres Straits the practice of mummification spread to Australia, as Flower (**19**), Frazer (**22**), Howitt (see Hertz, **33**), Roth (**71**) and Hamlyn-Harris (**28**), among others, have described. Roth says "Desiccation is a form of disposal of the dead practised only in the case of very distinguished men. After being disembowelled and dried by fire the corpse is tied up and carried about for months." (**71**, p. 393). The mummy was painted with red ochre (Fraser, **22**).

In Roth's photographs, as well as in the mummies which I have had the opportunity of examining, the embalming-incision was made in the characteristically Egyptian situation in the left flank. In one of the mummies in the Brisbane Museum (see **28**, plate 6) the head is severely damaged. Examination of the specimen indicates that incisions had been deliberately made. Perhaps it was an attempt to remove the brain, which ended in destruction of the cranium.

A curious feature of Australian embalming is that the body was always flexed, and not extended as in the Torres Straits. At first I was inclined to believe that this may be due to the influence of the Early Egyptian (Second Dynasty) procedure (**89**), but a fuller consideration of the evidence leads me to the conclusion that the adoption of the flexed position is due to syncretism with local burial customs, which were being observed when the bringers of the "heliolithic" culture reached Australia. It is probable that the boomerang came from Egypt, *viâ* East Africa, India (**12**) and Indonesia at the same time.

Several curious burial customs which may be regarded as degradations of the practice of mummification occur in Australia, but the consideration of these I must defer for the present.

In the discussion on Flower's memoir (**19**), Hyde Clarke justly emphasized "the importance of the demonstrations in reference to their bearings on the connection of the Australian populations with those of the main continents, and in the influence exerted in Australasia at a former time by a more highly cultivated race. This, to his mind, was the explanation of the relations of the higher culture, whether with regard to language, marriage and kindred, weapon names, or modes of culture, such as the mummies now described, the modes of incision, and form of burial. He did not consider these institutions, as some great authorities did, indigenous in Australia" (**19**, p. 394).

Corroborative evidence is now accumulating (**70**), which will definitely establish the reality of the influence thus adumbrated by Clarke 37 years ago.

Frazer (**22**, p. 80) says the burial (in Australia) on a raised stage reminds him of the "towers of silence," and adds: — "This novelty of a raised stage can scarcely be a thing which our blacks have invented for themselves since they came to Australia; and if it is a custom which some portion of their ancestors brought with them into this country, I would argue from it that these ancestors were once in contact with, or rather formed part of, a race which had beliefs similar to those of the Persians; such beliefs are not readily adopted by strangers; they belong to a race." Frazer proceeds to contrast this practice with the other Australian custom of desiccation, which, he says, "corresponds to the Egyptian practice of mummification" (p. 81): but, as Hertz (**33** *et supra*) has pointed out, they were inspired by the same fundamental idea, however much the present practitioners of the two methods may fail to realize this in their beliefs and traditions. The interesting suggestion emerges from these considerations that the peculiar Persian burial customs may be essentially a degraded and profoundly modified form of the ancient Egyptian funerary rites.

In his "Polynesian Researches" William Ellis (**15**) gives an interesting, though unfortunately too brief, account of the Tahitian practice of embalming. Among the poor and middle classes "methods of preservation were too expensive" to be used, but the body was "placed upon a sort of bier covered with the best native cloth" while awaiting burial (p. 399).

"The bodies of the dead, among the chiefs, were, however, in general preserved above ground: a temporary house or shed was erected for them, and they were placed on a kind of bier ... sometimes the moisture of the body was removed by pressing the different parts, drying it in the sun, and anointing it with fragrant oils. At other times, the intestines, brains, etcetera were removed: all moisture was extracted from the body, which was fixed in a sitting position during the day, and exposed to the sun, and, when placed horizontally at night was frequently turned over, that it might not remain long on the same side. The inside was then filled with cloth saturated with perfumed oils, which were also injected into other parts of the body, and carefully rubbed over the outside every day" (pp. 400 and 401).

"It was then clothed, and fixed in a sitting posture; a small altar was erected before it, and offerings of fruit, food and flowers, were daily presented by the relatives, or the priests appointed to attend the body. In this state it was preserved several months, and when it decayed, the skull was carefully kept by the family, while the other bones etc. were buried within the precincts of the family temple" (p. 401).

Ellis makes the significant comment:—"It is singular that the practice of preserving the bodies of their dead by the process of embalming, which has been thought to indicate a high degree of civilization, and which was carried to such perfection by one of the most celebrated nations of antiquity, some thousand years ago, should be found to prevail among this people." The whole of the circumstances attending the practice of this custom, and the curious ritual and the behaviour of the mourners, as described by Ellis, no less than the details of the process, in fact afford the most positive evidence of its derivation from Egypt.

Ellis says "it is also practiced by other distant nations of the Pacific, and on some of the coasts washed by its waters." "In some of the islands they dried the bodies, and, wrapping them in numerous folds of cloth, suspended them from the roofs of their dwelling-houses" (p. 406).

Ellis notes the remarkable points of identity between the Tahitian account of the deluge and not only the Hebrew but also those of the Mexicans and Peruvians and many other peoples (p. 394).

In Glaumont's summary (**24**, p. 517) five modes of burial are described as being practised in New Caledonia. The first is burial in the flexed position; 2nd, extended burial in caves; 3rd, exposure of the body in trees or on the mountains; 4th, mummification; 5th, the body erect or reposing in a dug-out canoe. With regard to the method of embalming, this is practised only in the case of a chief. The body of a chief soon after death was covered with pricks into which were introduced the juices of certain plants with the object of preventing decomposition of the tissues. Afterwards the body was suitably dried or smoked, then it was dressed in its best clothes, its face painted red and black, and then the body was preserved indefinitely. A hole was made at the top of the hut, and by means of this they haul up the mummy. After it has been exposed in this way for a certain time, the body was withdrawn from the hole into the house, which was then carefully shut up and became taboo with all that it contained. Analogous customs are found in New Zealand and elsewhere in Oceania. A singularly strange custom is now in use in the New Hebrides and in the Solomon Islands. The father and son, for example, or the husband and wife, having just died, they smoke the head alone as in New Zealand, but they make (with bamboo covered with cloth) a mannikin, having roughly the human form; then they tattoo the whole of the surface; fastened upon each shoulder—and this is the strange part of it—is a piece of bamboo, to one of which they attach the father's head and the other that of his son. [The account is not altogether intelligible here.] The heads are painted white and black. With reference to the placing of the body in a canoe, this is reserved for chiefs only. When a chief dies, messengers go in all directions, repeating "The sun is set." This expression springs from the idea that the chief is a god, the supreme Sun-god.

These procedures afford a remarkably complete series of links with the "heli-olithic" cult as practised elsewhere in the west and east. The account of the curious attachment of the heads to the shoulders of the dummy figure throw some light upon the custom (to which I have referred elsewhere in this communication) in Mallicolo (**61**, p. 138) and in America of representing human faces on the shoulders of such models. It is a remarkable fact that in certain of the Mallicolo figures the phallus is fixed to the girdle in a very curious manner, exactly analogous to that recently described and figured by Blackman from an Egyptian tomb of the Middle Kingdom at Meir.

Embalming was a method rarely employed in New Zealand.

"After the extraction of the softer parts, oil or salt was rubbed into the flesh, and the body was dried in the sun or over a fire; then the mummy was wrapped in cloth and hidden away."

"In some parts of New Zealand the skeletons of mummified bodies are found in the crouching or sitting posture" (Macmillan Brown, **7**, p. 70).

In Schmidt's *Jahrbücher der gesammten Medicin*, 1890, Bd. 226, p. 175, there is an abstract of an article on Samoa by P. Burzen in which, among other things, the three Egyptian operations of circumcision, massage and mummification are described as being practiced.

The embalming is done by women. After removing the viscera, which are buried or burnt, the eviscerated corpse is then soaked for two months in coconut oil, mixed with vegetable juices. When the body is fully treated and no more fluid escapes from it, the hair which had previously been cut off, is stuck on again with a resinous paste. The body cavity is packed with cloth soaked in vegetable oil and resinous materials: then the mummy is wrapped up with bandages, the head and hands being left exposed.

The body so prepared is put in a special place where it is preserved indefinitely.

"In Pitcairn Island 1,400 miles due west of Easter Island carved stone pillars or images of a somewhat similar character to those of Easter Island" are found (Enoch, **16**, p. 274).

"Another 1,400 miles to the north-west takes us to Tahiti. The natives of Tahiti buried their chiefs in temples; their embalmed bodies, after being exposed, were interred in a couching position. Mention is made of a pyramidal stone structure, on which were the actual altars, which stood at the farther end of one of the squares."

"There are many close analogies between the sacrificial practices and those of Mexico" (p. 275).

In their extensive migrations the carriers of the "heliolithic" culture took with them the custom of circumcision, and introduced it into most of the regions where their influence spread. In some of the areas affected by the "heliolithic" leaven the more primitive operation of "incision" is found. This consists not of removing the prepuce, but merely slitting up its dorsal aspect (**69**, p. 432). It was the method employed in Egypt in pre-dynastic times, when it was the custom to hide the phallus in a leather sheath suspended from a rope tied round the body. The practice of "incision" and the use of the pudendal sheath persists in some parts of Africa until the present day (see *Journ. Roy. Anthropol. Instit.* 1913, p. 120).

Rivers claims that "the practice of incision arose in Oceania as a modification of circumcision" (**69**, p. 436): but I think the possibility of it having been introduced from the west along with or before the practice of circumcision needs to be considered.

Another remarkable practice which probably formed part of the equipment of the heliolithic wanderers was massage. It was employed by the Egyptians as early as the Sixth Dynasty, as we know from the representations of the operations in a Sakkara *mastaba* (Capart, **11**). Piorry (**57**) has given an account of the wide range of the practice of massage, from Egypt to India, China and Tahiti, and the high state of efficiency attained in its use in ancient times in India and China. The Chinese manuscript *Kong-Fau* contained detailed accounts of the operation. Piorry remarks, "it is clear that for us its development did not originate from the practices described in the books of Cong-tzée or the compilation of Susrata."

From Rivers' interesting account of massage in Melanesia (**67**) it is evident that the method must have an origin common to it and the modern European practice, and that it could not have arisen amongst a barbarous people like the Melanesians, who have the most extraordinary conceptions as to why and how it serves a therapeutic purpose. Although we have no evidence to prove that massage spread along with the heliolithic culture, the fact that it has a similar geographical distribution, and certainly was extensively practised in Egypt long before the great migration began, suggests that it may represent another Egyptian element of that remarkable culture-complex.

In his masterly analysis of the cultures of Oceania (**69**) Rivers has given a useful summary of the evidence relating to the practice of preserving the body, and has drawn certain inferences from these and other burial practices, which I propose to examine. "In some cases, as in Tikopia, interment takes place either in the house or within a structure representing a house, while in Tonga and Samoa the bodies of chiefs are interred in vaults built of stone. Often the body is buried in a canoe or in a hollowed log of wood, which represents a canoe" (**69**, p. 269). From the evidence to which reference has been made in the course of the present memoir it is unnecessary to insist at any length on the importance and obvious significance of these facts. But I question the inference Rivers draws (p. 270) from the burial in boats. He says "the practice can be regarded as a result of the fact of migration, and does not show that the use of a canoe was the practice of the immigrants in their original home." The practice is so widespread, however, and in Egypt and elsewhere had such a deep-rooted significance that it is difficult to believe this custom was not brought by the immigrants with them. I am willing to admit that the special circumstances of the people of Oceania naturally emphasized what may be called the "boat-element" in the funerary ritual; but the association of the use of boats with burial is so curious and constant a feature of the "heliolithic" culture where-ever it manifests itself (*vide supra*) as hardly to have arisen independently in different parts of the area of distribution.

"A second mode of treatment is preservation of the body, either in the house or on a stage often covered with a roof. Some kind of mummification is usually practised in these cases, by continual rubbing with oil, drying by means of a fire, and puncture of the body to hasten the disappearance of the products of decomposition."

"In some parts of Samoa there is a definite process of embalming in which the viscera are removed and buried. A body thus treated lies on a platform resting upon a double canoe, and in many other places a canoe is used as a receptacle for the body while it is undergoing the process of mummification" (p. 269). This association of the use of a canoe with a method of preservation obviously Egyptian in origin naturally provokes comparison with the use of boats in the Egyptian funeral ceremonies. An instance is the boat found in the tomb of Amenophis II. (**81**). The platform is probably a type of bed found elsewhere in the region under consideration (see, for instance, Roth's account of the Queensland sleeping-platform) and represents the bier found so often elsewhere (*vide supra*). This is in no way inconsistent with Rivers' view that "exposure of the dead on platforms is only a survival of preservation in a house" (p. 273).

Earlier in this memoir I have explained why the Egyptians came to attach special importance to the head, and how the less cultured people of Africa, when faced with the difficulties of preserving the body, saved the skull (or in some cases the jaw). When it is recalled how widespread this custom is in other parts of the "heliolithic area," and how deep-rooted were the ideas which prompted so curious a procedure, Rivers' independent inference in regard to this matter is fully confirmed. "Many practices become intelligible as elements of a single culture if we suppose that a people imbued with the necessity for the preservation of the body after death acquired ... the further idea that the skull is the representative of the body as a whole; if they came to believe that the purpose for which they had hitherto preserved the body could be fulfilled as well if the head only were kept" (p. 273). This is unquestionably true: but I dissent from Rivers' qualification that this modification happened "perhaps in the course of their wanderings towards Oceania," because it has already been seen that it had occurred before the wanderers set out from the East African coast. There is, of course, the possibility that Africa may have been influenced by a cultural reflux from Indonesia, such as has been demonstrated in the case of Madagascar; but there are reasons for believing that the facts under consideration cannot be explained in this way.

In thus venturing upon criticisms of Rivers' great monograph I should like especially to emphasize the fact that these comments do not refer in any way to his attack on the "orthodox" ethnological position. On the contrary, the views that I am setting forth in this communication represent a further extension of Rivers' own attitude that the Oceanic cultures have been derived mainly from contacts with other peoples. A series of practices which he has hesitated to recognise as having been introduced, but inclined to regard as local developments, I hold to be part of the immigrant culture. The use of boats for burial, the custom of regarding the head as an efficient representative of the whole body and the practice of "incision" as well as circumcision (**69**, p. 432) are examples of customs, which he regards as local developments in the Pacific: but all three are equally distinctive of Ancient Egypt and occur at widely separated localities along the great "heliolithic" track. The linking-up of sun-worship with all the other elements of the "heliolithic cult" also compels me to question his limitation of such worship to certain regions only in Oceania (**69**, p. 549); even though I fully admit that the data used by Rivers are not sufficient to justify any further inference than he has drawn from them.

My aim is then, not an attempt to weaken Rivers' general attitude, but enormously to strengthen it, by demonstrating that each culture-complex was brought into the Pacific in an even more complete form than he had postulated. Nor does my criticism affect his hypothesis of a series of cultural waves into Oceania. Here, again, I am prepared to go not only the whole way with him, but even further, and to seek for additional cultural influences which he has not yet defined.

Most modern writers who refer in any way to the preserved bodies which have been found in vast numbers in Peru and in other parts of America assume that these bodies have been preserved not by embalming or any other artificial method or mode of treatment, but simply as the result of desiccation by the unaided forces of nature. Although in the great majority of cases there are no obvious signs of any artificial means having been employed to preserve the bodies, yet a not inconsiderable number of examples have come to light to demonstrate the reality of the practice of mummification in America (**3**; **37**; **58**; **63**; and **106**). Yarrow's classical monograph (**106**) established the reality of the practice of embalming in America quite conclusively. Moreover the fact that practically every item of the multitude of curiously distinctive practices found widespread in other parts of the world, in the most intimate association with methods of embalming certainly inspired by Egypt, puts it beyond all reasonable doubt that the variety of American practices for preserving the body is also to be attributed to the same source.

In his book on the "History of the Conquest of Peru," Prescott makes the following statement:—"When an Inca died (or, to use his own language, was called home to the mansion of his father, the Sun) his obsequies were celebrated with great pomp and solemnity. The bowels were taken from the body and deposited in the Temple of Tampu, about five leagues from the capital. A quantity of his plate and jewels was buried with him, and a number of his attendants and favourite concubines, amounting sometimes, it is said, to a thousand, were immolated on his tomb....

"The body of the deceased Inca was skilfully embalmed and removed to the great Temple of the Sun at Cuzco. There the Peruvian sovereign on entering the awful sanctuary might behold the effigies of his royal ancestors, ranged in opposite files—the men on the right and their queens on the left of the great luminary which blazed in refulgent gold on the walls of the temple. The bodies, clothed in princely attire which they had been accustomed to wear, were placed on chairs of gold, and sat with their heads inclined downwards, their hands placidly crossed over their bosoms, their countenances exhibiting their natural dusky hue—less liable to change than the fresher colouring of a European complexion—and their hair of raven black, or silvered over with age, according to the period at which they died. It seemed like a company of solemn worshippers fixed in devotion, so true were the forms and lineaments to life. The Peruvians were as successful as the Egyptians in the miserable attempt to perpetuate the existence of the body beyond the limits assigned to it by nature. [Note—Ondegardo, Rel. Prim., M.S.—Garcilasso, Com. Real., parte i., lib. v., cap. xxix. The Peruvians secreted their mummies of their sovereigns after the Conquest, that they might not be profaned by the insults of the Spaniards. Ondegardo, when corregidor of Cuzco, discovered five of them, three males and two females. The former were the bodies of Viracocha, of the great Tupac, Inca Yupanqui, and of his son, Huayna Cupac. Garcilasso saw them in 1650. They were dressed in their regal robes, with no insignia but the llautu on their heads. They were in a sitting position, and, to use his own expression, 'perfect as life, without so much as a hair of an eyebrow wanting.' As they were carried through the streets, decently shrouded with a mantle, the Indians threw themselves on their knees, in sign of reverence, with many tears and groans, and were still more touched as they beheld some of the Spaniards themselves doffing their caps in token of respect to departed royalty. (*Ibid. ubi supra.*) The bodies were subsequently removed to Lima; and Father Acosta, who saw them there some twenty years later, speaks of them as still in perfect preservation]" (**58**, pp. 19 and 20).

Later on in the same work Prescott, relying again on the somewhat, questionable authority of Garcilasso's works, makes a statement which in some respects may seem to be at variance with what I have just quoted:—

"It was this belief in the resurrection of the body which led them to preserve the body with so much solicitude—by a simple process, however, that unlike the elaborate embalming of the Egyptians, consisted in exposing it to the action of the cold, exceedingly dry and highly rarified atmosphere of the mountains. [Note.—Such indeed seems to be the opinion of Garcilasso, though some writers speak of resinous and other applications for embalming the body. The appearance of the royal mummies found at Cuzco, as reported both by Ondegardo and Garcilasso, makes it probable that no foreign substance was employed for their preservation.] As they believed that the occupations in the future world would have great resemblance to those of the present, they buried with the deceased noble some of his apparel, his utensils, and frequently his treasures; and completed the gloomy ceremony by sacrificing his wives and favourite domestics to bear him company and do him service in the happy regions beyond the clouds. Vast mounds of an irregular or more frequently oblong shape, penetrated by galleries running at right angles to each other were raised over the dead, whose dried bodies or mummies have been found in considerable numbers, sometimes erect, but more often in the sitting posture common to the Indian tribes of both continents" (p. 54).

In the light of the information concerning the practices in other parts of the world, which I have collected in the present memoir, there can be no doubt of the substantial accuracy of these reports, and that they refer to real embalming and not to mere natural desiccation.

Hrdlička has adduced positive evidence of the adoption of embalming procedures (**37**).

In his report, "Culture of the Ancient Pueblos of the Upper Gila River Region, New Mexico and Arizona," Walter Hough (**36**) publishes excellent photographs of two mummies of babies, but he gives no information as to the method of preservation.

There are four Peruvian mummies in the Anatomical Museum in the University of Manchester, three of which are adults, and one of them a baby. In only one of them is there any positive evidence of artificial measures having been adopted for the preservation of the body, and in this case the condition of the mummy was a most amazing one. The body was clad in woollen garments in the usual way, and was wearing a woollen peaked cap, the apex of which was furnished with a bunch of feathers. The body was placed in a sitting position, and a large wound extending across the trunk had been covered with cloth strongly impregnated with resinous material. The legs were sharply flexed upon the body and the arms were bound up in front. But to my intense amazement I found the shoulder blades on the front of the chest, and on examination found that the thorax was turned back to front. As the head was already separate there was nothing to show what position it originally occupied; and it seemed impossible to explain how it had been possible to twist the vertebral column in the lumbar region as to bring the thorax back to front. In order to solve this mystery I removed the resin-impregnated cloth, which was firmly fixed to the abdominal wound, and found that the body had been cut right across the abdomen and packed with wool after the viscera had been removed. Then the abdomen and thorax had been stuck together by means of the broad strip of cloth with resinous paste as an adhesive. But for some reason which is not very apparent, or probably through mere carelessness, the thorax had been placed the wrong way round, and it had become necessary, in order to restore some semblance of life-like appearance to the monstrosity, forcibly to twist the arms at the shoulder joints in order to get them into the position above described. [Since this was written I have learned that in certain American tribes it is the custom to dress the corpse with a coat turned back to front. This seems to suggest that the curious procedure just described may have been dictated by the same underlying idea, whatever it may be.] In the cranium of this case the remains of the desiccated brain were still present, and although there was a quantity of brownish powder along with it, the evidence was not sufficiently definite to say whether or not any foreign material had been introduced into the cranial cavity. In the case of the other three bodies, as I have already mentioned, there was no evidence, apart from the excellent state of preservation, to suggest what measures had been taken to hinder the process of decomposition.

In his account of the obsequies of the Aztec kings, Bancroft (**3**, Vol. II., p. 603) tells us that "the body was washed with aromatic water, extracted chiefly from trefoil, and occasionally a process of embalming was resorted to. The bowels were taken out and replaced by aromatic substances." "The art was an ancient one, however, dating from the Toltecs as usual, yet generally known and practised throughout the whole country" (p. 604). He then proceeds to describe "a curious mode of preserving bodies used by the lord of Chalco," which consisted of desiccation; and adds a singularly interesting reference to libations, not only curiously reminiscent of the ancient Egyptian practice, but also described in language which might be regarded as a paraphrase of the Pyramid text expounded by Blackman (**5**). "Water was then poured upon its [the mummy's] head with these words: 'this is the water which thou usedst in this world'—Brasseur de Bourbourg uses the expression 'C'est cette eau que tu as reçue en venant au monde'" (Bancroft, **3**, Vol. II., p. 604).

It is altogether inconceivable that such a curious practice, embodying so remarkable an idea, could by chance have been invented independently in Egypt and in America. This can be no mere coincidence, but proof of the most definite kind of the derivation of these Toltec and Aztec ideas from Egypt.

Bancroft further describes (**3**, p. 604 *et seq.*) a whole series of other ritual observances, many of which find close parallels in the scenes depicted in the royal Egyptian tombs of the New Empire.

I have already referred to Tylor's case (**102**) of the adoption *in toto* by the Aztecs of the Japanese Buddhist's story of the soul's wanderings in the spirit-land. In the case recorded by Bancroft almost the same story is reproduced, but with the characteristic Egyptian additions relating to parts of the way guarded by a gigantic snake and an alligator respectively [in the Egyptian ritual it is of course the Crocodile; see Budge, "The Egyptian Heaven and Hell," Vol. 1, p. 159]. This is a most remarkable example of syncretism between the Egyptian ritual of the New Empire with Buddhist practices on the distant shores of America.

As the connecting link between the Old and New World, it may be noted that in Oceania "everywhere is the belief that the soul after death must undertake a journey, beset with various perils, to the abode of departed spirits, which is usually represented as lying towards the west" (**61**, p. 138).

Reutter (**63**) gives a summary of information relating to the practice of embalming in the New World and particularly amongst the Incas. The custom of preserving the body was not general in every case, for amongst certain peoples only the bodies of kings and chiefs were embalmed. The Indian tribes of Virginia, of North Carolina, the Congarees of South Carolina, the Indians of the North-West Coast, of Central America and those of Florida practised this custom as well as the Incas. In Florida the body was dried before a big fire, then it was clothed in rich materials and afterwards it was placed in a special niche in a cave where the relatives and friends used to come on special days and converse with the deceased. According to Beverley (1722) the tribes of Virginia practised embalming in the following way:—The skin was incised from the head to the feet and the viscera as well as the soft parts of the body were removed. To prevent the skin from drying up and becoming brittle oil and other fatty materials were applied to it. In Kentucky when the body had been dried and filled with fine sand it was wrapped in skins or in matting and buried either in a cave or in a hut. In Colombia the inhabitants of Darien used to remove the viscera and fill the body cavity with resin, afterwards they smoked the body and preserved it in their houses reposing either in a hammock or in a wooden coffin. The Muiscas, the Aleutians, the inhabitants of Yucatan and Chiapa also embalmed the bodies of their kings, of their chiefs, and of their priests by methods similar to those just described, with modifications varying from tribe to tribe. Reutter acknowledges as the source of most of his information the memoirs of Bauwenns, entitled "Inhumation et Cremation," and Parcelly, "Étude Historique et Critique des Embaumements"; but most of it has clearly been obtained from Yarrow's great monograph (**106**). Alone amongst the people of the New World who practised embalming the Incas employed it not only for their kings, chiefs and priests, but also for the population in general. These people were not confined to Peru, but dwelt also in Bolivia, in Equador, as well as in a part of Chili and of the Argentine. Mummified bodies were placed in monuments called Chullpas. According to De Morcoy these Chullpas were constructed of unbaked brick and were sometimes built in the form of a truncated pyramid, twenty to thirty feet high, in other cases simple mausolea of a simple monolith. The burial chamber inside them was square and as many as a dozen mummies might be buried in a single one. The bodies were sharply flexed and were placed in a sitting position. An interesting and curious fact about these mummies, or at any rate those from Upper Peru, was that all of them presented on the forehead or on the occiput a circle composed of small holes through the wall of the cranium, which had probably been used for evacuating the brain and for the introduction of preservative substances.

Yarrow (**106**) refers to the fact that the Indians of the North-West coast and the Aleutian Islands also embalm their dead. This, like the practice of tattooing (Buckland, **10**), serves to map out the possible alternative northern route taken by the spread of culture from Asia to America (*vide supra* the account of Aino embalming; also *Map II.*).

In his account of the Araucanos of Southern Chile (*Journ. Roy. Anthr. Inst.*, Vol. 39, 1909, p. 364) Latcham describes how, when a person of importance dies of disease, these people believe that some one must have poisoned him. They "open the side of the deceased" and extract the gall-bladder, so as to obtain from the bile contained in it some clue as to the guilty person. "The corpse is then hung in a wicker frame and under it a fire is kept smouldering till such time as the perpetrator be found and punished."

This confused jumble of practices suggestive of a blending of the influences of Egyptian embalming and Babylonian hepatoscopy is also obviously linked to the customs of Oceania and Indonesia.

Scattered in certain protected localities along the whole extent of the great "heliolithic" track the ancient Egyptian [also Chaldean and Indian] practice of burial in large urns or jars occurs. In America also it is found; but, according to Yarrow, it is restricted to certain people of New Mexico and California, although similar urns have been found in Nicaragua.

After the coming of the first great "heliolithic" wave, Asiatic civilization did not cease to influence America.

There are innumerable signs of the later effects of both Western and Eastern Asiatic developments. For instance, there is the coming of the practice of cremation. The fact that such burial customs are spread sporadically in the islands of the Pacific suggests that the custom may have been carried to America by the same route as the main stream of the "heliolithic" cult; but against this is the evidence that cremation was practised especially on the Pacific slope of the Rocky Mountains, and in Mexico rather than in Peru. It seems more probable that the main stream of the later wave of culture, of which cremation is the most distinctive practice, took the northern route skirting the eastern Asiatic littoral and then following the line of the Aleutian Islands.

In the account of the method of mummification adopted by the Virginian Indians (*supra*) it was seen that the whole skin was removed and afterwards fitted on to the skeleton again. Great care and skill had to be used to prevent the skin shrinking. Apparently the difficulties of this procedure led certain Indian tribes to give up the attempt to prevent the skin shrinking. Thus the Jivaro Indians of Ecuador, as well as certain tribes in the western Amazon area, make a practice of preserving the head only, and, after removing the skull, allowing the softer tissues to shrink to a size not much bigger than a cricket ball (**44**; **52**, p. 252, and **61**, p. 288).

According to Page (**52**), who has described one of the two Jivaro specimens now in the Manchester Museum, desiccation by heat was the method of preservation. He adds, "'Momea' and 'Chancha' are the names commonly given to such specimens by the natives." Surely the former must be a Spanish importation!

A comparison of this variety in the methods of preserving the body in America with the series of similar practices which I have been following from the African shore, makes it abundantly plain that there can be no doubt as to the source of the American inspiration to do such extraordinary things. The remarkable burial ritual and all the associated procedures afford strong corroborative evidence.

But the proof of the influence of the civilizations of the Old World on pre-Columbian America does not depend upon the evidence of one set of practices, however complex, bizarre and distinctive they may be.

The positive demonstration that I have endeavoured to build up in this communication depends upon the fact that the whole of the complex structure of the "heliolithic" culture, which was slowly built up in Egypt during the course of the thirty centuries before 900 B.C., spread to the east, acquiring on its way accretions from the civilizations of the Mediterranean, Western Asia, Eastern Africa, India, Eastern Asia and Indonesia and Oceania, until it reached America. Like a potent ferment it gradually began to leaven the vast and widespread aboriginal culture of the Americas.

The rude megalithic architecture of America bears obvious evidences of the same inspiration which prompted that of the Old World; and so far as the more sumptuous edifices are concerned the primary stimulus of Egyptian ideas, profoundly modified by Babylonian, and to a less extent Indian and Eastern Asiatic, influences is indubitable. Comparison of the truncated pyramids of America, of the Pacific, Eastern Asia and Indonesia with those of ancient Chaldea, affords quite definite corroboration of these views. It would be idle to pretend that so complex a design and so strange a symbolism as the combination of the sun's disc with the serpent and the greatly expanded wings of a hawk, carved upon the lintel of the door of a temple of the sun, could possibly have developed independently in Ancient Egypt and in Mexico (see especially Bancroft, **3**, Vol. IV., p. 351).

But it is not merely the designs of the buildings and their association with the practice of mummification (and later, in Mexico, with cremation), but the nature of the cult of the temples and all the traditions associated with them that add further corroboration. Thus, for example, Wake (**103**, p. 383), describing the geographical distribution of serpent-worship (the intimate bond of which with sun-worship and in fact the whole "heliolithic" cult was forged in Egypt, as I have already explained), writes:—"Quetzalcoatl, the divine benefactor of the Mexicans, was an incarnation of the serpent-sun Tonacatlcoatl, who thus became the great father, as the female serpent Cihuacoatl was the great mother, of the human race." "The solar character of the serpent-god appears to be placed beyond all doubt.... The kings and priests of ancient peoples claimed this divine origin, and 'children of the sun' was the title of the members of the sacred caste. When the actual ancestral character of the deity is hidden he is regarded as 'the father of his people' and their divine benefactor. He is the introducer of agriculture, the inventor of arts and sciences, and the civilizer of mankind."

Writing of the Maya empire, Bancroft (**3**, Vol. V., p. 233) says:—"The Plumed Serpent, known in different tongues as Quetzalcoatl, Gucumatz, and Cukulcan, was the being who traditionally founded the new order of things."

Even the most trivial features of the "heliolithic" culture-complex make their appearance in America. Thus, for example, Harrison tells us that:—

"The artificial enlargement of the lobe [of the ear] appears originally to have been adopted in India for the purpose of receiving a solar disc" (**29**, p. 193).

"The early Spanish historian mentioned that an elaborate religious ceremony took place in the temple of the Sun at Cuzco, on the occasion of boring the ears of the young Peruvian nobles" (p. 196).

"The practice of enlarging the ear lobes was connected with Sun-worship" (p. 198).

So also in the case of circumcision, tattooing, and almost every one of the curious customs I have enumerated in the foregoing account. Then, again, all the characteristic stories of the creation, the deluge, the petrifaction of human beings and of spirits dwelling in rocks, and of the origin of the chosen people from an incestuous union make their appearance in Mexico, Peru and elsewhere.

The peculiar Swastika symbol, associated with the "heliolithic" cult by pure chance in the place of its origin, which the people of Timor, in Indonesia, regard as the ancient emblem of fire, the Son of the Sun, also appears in America.

Even so bizarre a practice as the artificial deformation of the head (**48**, pp. 515 to 519), which seems to have originated in Armenia, became added to the repertoire of the fantastic collection of tricks of the "heliolithic" wanderers, and was adopted sporadically by numerous isolated groups of people along the great migration route. For some reason this strange idea "caught on" in America to a greater extent than elsewhere and spread far and wide throughout the greater part of the continent.

Many other curious customs might be cited as straws that indicate clearly which way the stream of culture has flowed. For instance Keane (**42**, p. 264) states that "like the Burmese the Nicobarese place a piece of money in the mouth of a corpse before burial to help it in the other world"; and Hutchinson (**38**, p. 448) supplies the link across the Pacific: — "Men, women and children [in ancient Peru] had frequently a bit of copper between the teeth, like the obolus which the pagan Romans used to place in the mouth to pay ferry to the boatman Charon for passage across the Styx."

This reference to Charon reminds us also of the widespread custom, apparently originating in Egypt and spread far and wide, right out into the Pacific and America, of the association of a boat with the funerary ritual, to ferry the mummy to the west.

Certain distinctive aspects of phallism in America might also be mentioned as evidence of the influence of Old World practices.

In the appendix (part 1) to his "Conquest of Mexico," Prescott (**59**) summarises fully and fairly the large and highly suggestive mass of evidence available at the time when he wrote in favour of the view that the pre-Columbian civilization of Mexico and Peru had been inspired from Asia. In view of the apparent conclusiveness of his statement of the evidence it becomes a matter of some interest and importance to enquire into the reasons which, in the face of the apparently overwhelming testimony of the facts he has summarised, restrained him from adopting the obvious conclusion to which his whole argument points.

Referring to the numerous islands of the Pacific as one means of access of population to America, Prescott quotes Cook's voyages to illustrate how easily the Polynesians travelled from island to island hundreds of miles apart, and adds, "it would be strange if these wandering barks should not sometimes have been intercepted by the great continent, which stretches across the globe, in unbroken continuity, almost from pole to pole.

"Whence did the refinement of these more polished races [of America] come? Was it only a higher development of the same Indian character, which we see, in the more northern latitudes, defying every attempt at permanent civilization? Was it engrafted on a race of higher order in the scale originally, but self-instructed, working its way upward by its own powers? Was it, in short, an indigenous civilization? or was it borrowed, in some degree, from the nations of the Eastern world? If indigenous, how are we to explain the singular coincidence with the

East in institutions and opinions? If Oriental, how shall we account for the great dissimilarity in language, and for the ignorance of some of the most simple and useful arts, which, once known, it would seem scarcely possible should have been forgotten? This is the riddle of the Sphinx, which no Œdipus has yet had the ingenuity to solve."

In the light of the facts brought together in the present memoir, it requires no Œdipus to answer the riddle. For the only two objections which Prescott raises in opposition to the great mass of evidence he cites in favour of the derivation of American civilization from the Old World can easily be disposed of. Rivers has completely disposed of one by his demonstration of the fact that people—moreover those on the direct route across the Pacific to America—do actually "forget simple and useful arts" (**65**). The other objection is equally easily disposed of, when it is remembered that it requires only a few people of higher culture to leaven a large mass of lower culture with the elements of a higher civilization (see also on this point, Rivers, **68**). Moreover, if language is made a test, the affinities of the various American tribes one with the other would have to be denied. Thus, the language difficulty cuts both ways. But when we have disposed of his objections, the whole of his admirable summary then becomes valid as an argument in favour of the derivation of American culture from Asia across the Pacific.

Since then it has become the fashion on the part of most ethnologists either contemptuously to put aside the probability or even the possibility of the derivation of American civilization from the Old World (characteristic examples of this attitude will be found in Fewkes' address, **18**, and Keane's text-book, **41**). On the other side the discussion has been seriously compromised from time to time by a wholly uncritical and often recklessly inexact use of the evidence in support of the reality of the contact, which has to some extent prejudiced the serious discussion of the problem. Perhaps the least objectionable of such unfortunate attempts are Macmillan Brown's (**7**) and Enoch's books (**16**). The former has been led astray by grotesque errors in chronology and the failure to realize that useful arts can be lost. Enoch, on the other hand, has collected a large series of interesting but incompatible statements, and has made no serious attempt to sift or assimilate them.

But from time to time serious students, proceeding with the caution befitting the discussion of so difficult a problem, have definitely expressed their adherence to the view that elements of culture did spread across, or around, the Pacific from Asia to America (**8**; **9**; **10**; **15**; **20**; **21**; **29**; **30**; **38**; **48**; **49**; **50**; **51**; **60**; **73**; **102**; **103** and **105**). Among modern demonstrations I would especially call attention to the evidence collected by Dall (**73**, p. 395), Cyrus Thomas (**73**, p. 396), Tylor (**102**) and Zelia Nuttall (**49** and **50**), and of the older literature the remarkable statement of Ellis (**15**, p. 117). [In Mrs. Nuttall's monograph (**49**) there is a great deal, especially in the introductory part, to which serious objection must be taken: but in spite of the strong bias in favour of "psychological explanation" with which she started, eventually she was compelled to admit the force of the evidence for the spread of culture.]

For detailed statements concerning the discussions of this problem in the past the reader is referred to Bancroft's excellent summary (**3**), which also supplies a wonderfully rich storehouse of facts and traditions wholly corroborative of the conclusions at which I have arrived in the present memoir.

I find it difficult to conceive how there could ever have been any doubt about the matter on the part of anyone who knows his "Bancroft."

It will naturally be asked, if the case in proof of the actual diffusion of culture from Asia to America is so overwhelmingly convincing, on what grounds is assent refused? One school (of which the most characteristic utterance that I know of is Fewkes' presidential address, **18**) refuses to discuss the evidence: with pontifical solemnity it lays down the dogma of independent evolution as an infallible principle which it is almost sacrilege to question. I can best illustrate the methods of the other school of reactionaries by a sample of its dialectic.

No single incident in the discussion of the origin of American civilization has given rise to greater consternation in the ranks of the "orthodox" ethnologists than Tylor's statement (**102**):—

"The conception of weighing in a spiritual balance in the judgment of the dead, which makes its earliest appearance in the Egyptian religion, was traced thence into a series of variants, serving to draw lines of intercourse through the Vedic and Zoroastrian religions, extending from Eastern Buddhism to Western Christendom. The associated doctrine of the Bridge of the Dead, which separates the good, who pass over, from the wicked, who fall into the abyss, appears first in ancient Persian religion, reaching in like manner to the extremities of Asia and Europe. By these mythical beliefs historical ties are practically constituted, connecting the great religions of the world, and serving as lines along which their interdependence is to be followed out. Evidence of the same kind was brought forward in support of the theory, not sufficiently recognised by writers on culture history, of the Asiatic influences under which the pre-Columbian culture of America took shape. In the religion of old Mexico four great scenes in the journey of the soul in the land of the dead are mentioned by early Spanish writers after the conquest, and are depicted in a group in the Aztec picture-writing known as the Vatican Codex. The four scenes are, first, the crossing of the river; second, the fearful passage of the soul between the two mountains which clash together; third, the soul's climbing up the mountain set with sharp obsidian knives; fourth, the dangers of the wind carrying such knives on its blast. The Mexican pictures of these four scenes were compared with more or less closely corresponding pictures representing scenes from the Buddhist hells or purgatories as depicted on Japanese temple scrolls. Here, first, the river of death is shown, where the souls wade across; second, the souls have to pass between two huge iron mountains, which are pushed together by two demons; third, the guilty souls climb the mountain of knives, whose blades cut their hands and feet; fourth, fierce blasts of wind drive against their lacerated forms, the blades of knives flying through the air. It was argued that the appearance of analogues so close and complex of Buddhist ideas in Mexico constituted a correspondence of so high an order as to preclude any explanation except direct transmission from one religion to another. The writer, referring also to Humboldt's argument from the calendars and mythic catastrophes in Mexico and Asia, and to the correspondence in Bronze Age work and in games in both regions, expressed the opinion that on these cumulative proofs anthropologists might well feel justified in treating the nations of America as having reached their level of culture under Asiatic influence."

One might have imagined that such an instance, especially when backed with the authority[18] of our greatest anthropologist, who certainly has no bias in favour of the views I am promulgating, would have carried conviction to the mind of anyone willing to be convinced by precise evidence. But not to Mr. Keane! In endeavouring to whittle down the significance of this crucial case, he incidentally illustrates the lengths of unreason to which this school of ethnologists will push their argument, when driven to formulate a *reductio ad absurdum* without realizing the magnitude of the absurdity their blind devotion to a catch-word impels them to perpetrate.

In Keane's "Ethnology" (**41**, pp. 217-219) the following passages are found:—

"It is further to be noticed that religious ideas, like social usages, are easily transmitted from tribe to tribe, from race to race. [Most of my critics base their opposition on a denial of these very assumptions!] Hence resemblances in this order, where they arise, must rank very low as ethnical tests. If not the product of a common cerebral structure, they can prove little beyond social contact in remote or later times. A case in point is [Tylor's statement, which I have just quoted].

"The parallelism is complete; but the range of thought is extremely limited — nothing but mountains and knives, beside the river of death common to Egyptians, Greeks, and all peoples endowed with a little imagination." "Hence Prof. E. B. Tylor, who calls attention to the points of resemblance, builds far too much on them when he adduces them as convincing evidence of pre-Columbian culture in America taking shape under Asiatic influences. In the same place he refers to Humboldt's argument based on the similarity of calendars and of mythical catastrophes. But the 'mythical catastrophes,' floods and the like, have long been discounted, while the Mexican calendar, despite the authority of Humboldt's name, presents no resemblance whatsoever to those of the 'Tibetan and Tartar tribes,' or to any other of the Asiatic calendars with which it has been compared. 'There is absolutely no similarity between the Tibetan calendar and the primitive form of the American,' which, 'was not intended as a year-count, but as a ritual and formulary,' and whose signs 'had nothing to do with the signs of the zodiac, as had all those of the Tibetan and Tartar calendars' (D. G. Brinton, 'On various supposed Relations between the American and Asian races,' from *Memoirs of the International Congress of Anthropology*, Chicago, p. 148). Regarding all such analogies as may exist 'between the culture and customs of Mexico and those of China, Cambodia, Assyria, Chaldæa, and Asia Minor,' Dr. Brinton asks pertinently, 'Are we, therefore, to transport all these ancient peoples, or representatives of them, into Mexico?' (*ib.* p, 147). So Lefevre, who regards as 'quite chimerical' the attempts made to trace such resemblances to the Old World. 'If there are coincidences, they are fortuitous, or they result from evolution, which leads all the human group through the same stages and by the same steps' ('Race and Language,' p. 185).

"Many far more inexplicable coincidencies than any of those here referred to

[18] For the whole driving force of the so-called "psychological" ethnologists is really a reverence for authority and a meaningless creed.

occur in different regions, where not even contact can be suspected. Such is the strange custom of *Couvade*, which is found to prevail among peoples so widely separated as the Basques and Guiana Indians, who could never have either directly or indirectly in any way influenced each other" (**34**).

It is surely unnecessary to comment at length upon this quibbling, which is a fair sample of the kind of self-destructive criticism one meets in ethnological discussions nowadays. Talking of the "limitation of the range of thought" when out of the unlimited possibilities for its unhampered activities the human mind hit upon four episodes of such a fantastic nature, Keane taxes the credulity of his readers altogether too much when he solemnly tries to persuade them that such ideas are the most natural things in the world for mankind to imagine!

Surely it would have been better tactics frankly to admit the identity of origin, and then, following the example of Hough (**35**), minimize its importance by indicating the variety of possible ways by which Asiatic influence may have influenced America sporadically in comparatively recent times.

But instead of this, Keane insisted upon pushing his refusal to admit the most obvious inferences to the extreme limit and invoked the practice of *Couvade* as the *coup de grâce* to the views he was criticizing. But it was singularly unfortunate for his argument that he selected *Couvade*. His dogmatic assertion that the two peoples he selected are "so widely separated" that they could "never have either directly or indirectly in any way influenced one another" is entirely controverted by the fact that, although *Couvade* is, or was, a widespread custom, all the places where it occurred are either within the main route of the great "heliolithic culture-wave" or so near as easily to be within its sphere of influence. Thus it is recorded among the Basques,[19] in Africa, India, the Nicobar Islands, Borneo, China, Peru, Mexico, Central California, Brazil and Guiana. Instead of being a "knockout blow" to the view I am maintaining, the geographical distribution of this singularly ludicrous practice is a very welcome addition to the list of peculiar baggage which the "heliolithic" traveller carried with him in his wanderings, and a striking confirmation of the fact that in the spread from its centre of origin this custom must have travelled along the same route as the other practices we are examining.

After the artificialities of Keane and Fewkes, it is a satisfaction to turn back to the writings of the old ethnologists who lived in the days before the so-called "psychological" and "evolutionary explanations" were invented, and were content to accept the obvious interpretation of the known facts.

More than eighty years ago, Ellis (**15**, p. 117) with remarkable insight explained the relationships of the Polynesians and their wanderings, from Western Asia to America, with a lucidity and definiteness which must excite the enthusiastic admiration of those familiar with the fuller information now available. On p. 119 he cites an interesting series of racial factors, usages and beliefs in substantiation of the cultural link between the Pacific Islands and America.

Quite apart from the mere evidence provided by the arts, customs and beliefs in favour of the transmission of certain of the essential elements of American civi-

---

[19] Recent literature has thrown some doubt upon its occurrence in Western Europe.

lization from the Old World, there is a considerable amount of evidence of another kind, consisting no doubt to a large extent of mere scraps. For instance, there are not only the stories of Chinese and Japanese junks arriving on the American shore and of American traditions of the coming of pale-faced bearded men from the east,[20] but there is also a certain amount of evidence from the physical characters of the population themselves. It has been raised as an objection by many people that if there had been any considerable emigration of Polynesians into America they would have left a much more definite trace of their coming in the physical characters of the people of America than is supposed the case. But this argument does not necessarily carry very much weight, for the number of such Polynesians who reached America would have been a mere drop in the ocean of the vast aboriginal population of the Americas. Moreover, there is a certain amount of evidence of the presence of people with Polynesian traits in certain parts of the Pacific littoral. Von Humboldt stated the people of Mexico and Peru had much larger beards and moustaches than the rest of the Indians. But there is a more striking instance in substantiation of the reality of this mixture of Pacific people in America which raises the possibility that a certain number of Melanesians, whose physical characters, being more obtrusive by contrast than those of the Polynesians, were more easily detected. In Allen's memoir (**2**, p. 47) the following statements are found: —

"Sir Arthur Helps tells us in his 'History of Spanish Conquest in America' that the Spaniards, when they first visited Darien under Vasco Nunez, found there a race of black men, whom they (gratuitously as it seems to me) supposed to be descended from a cargo of shipwrecked negroes; this race was living distinct from the other races and at enmity with them,"

and on page 48,

"Perhaps other black tribes may be discovered upon a more careful enquiry, and if the theory of Crawford be accepted, which represents the inhabitants of Polynesia in Ante-historic times as being a great semi-civilized nation who had made some progress in agriculture and understood the use of gold and iron, were clothed 'with a fabric made of the fibrous bark of plants which they wove in the loom,' and had several domesticated animals, a new and unexpected light may possibly be thrown upon the origin of primitive American culture. It is certain that massive ruins and remains of pyramidal structures and terraced buildings closely analogous to those of India, Java and Cambodia, as well as to those of Central America, Mexico and Peru, exist in many islands of Polynesia, such as the Ladrone Islands, Tahiti, Fiji, Easter Island and the Sandwich Islands, and the customs of the Polynesians are almost all of them found to exist also amongst the American races."

"Perhaps here, then, we have the 'missing link' between the Old World civilizations and the mysterious civilizations of America."

---

[20] It is quite possible this may refer to the relatively modern incursion of Norsemen and other Europeans into America by the North Atlantic.

SUMMARY.

Between 4000 B.C. and 900 B.C. a highly complex culture compounded of a remarkable series of peculiar elements, which were associated the one with the other in Egypt largely by chance, became intimately interwoven to form the curious texture of a cult which Brockwell has labelled "heliolithic," in reference to the fact that it includes sun-worship, the custom of building megalithic monuments, and certain extraordinary beliefs concerning stones. An even more peculiar and distinctive feature, genetically related to the development of megalithic practices and the belief that human beings could dwell in stones, is the custom of mummification.

The earliest known Egyptians (before 4000 B.C.) practised weaving and agriculture, performed the operation of "incision" (the prototype of complete circumcision), and probably were sun-worshippers. Long before 3400 B.C. they began to work copper and gold. By 3000 B.C. they had begun the practice of embalming, making rock-cut tombs, stone superstructures and temples. By the mere chance that the capital of the united Kingdom of Egypt happened to be in the centre of serpent-worship (and the curious symbolism associated with it—Sethe, **74**), the sun, serpent and Horus-hawk (the older symbol of royalty) became blended in the symbol of sun-worship and as the emblem of the king, who was regarded as the son of the sun-god.

The peculiar beliefs regarding the possibility of animate beings dwelling in stone statues (and later even in uncarved columns), and of human beings becoming petrified, developed out of the Egyptian practices of the Pyramid Age (circa 2800 B.C.).

By 900 B.C. practically the whole of the complex structure of the "heliolithic" culture had become built up and definitely conventionalized in Egypt, with numerous purely accidental additions from neighbouring countries.

The great migration of the "heliolithic" culture-complex probably began shortly before 800 B.C. [Its influence in the Mediterranean and in Europe, as also in China and Japan, is merely mentioned incidentally in this communication.]

Passing to the east the culture-complex reached the Persian Gulf strongly tainted with the influence of North Syria and Asia Minor, and when it reached the west coast of India and Ceylon, possibly as early as the end of the eighth century B.C., it had been profoundly influenced not only by these Mediterranean, Anatolian and especially Babylonian accretions, but even more profoundly with Eastern African modifications. These Ethiopian influences become more pronounced in Indonesia (no doubt because in India and the west the disturbances created by other cults have destroyed most of the evidence).

From Indonesia the "heliolithic" culture-complex was carried far out into the Pacific and eventually reached the American coast, where it bore fruit in the development of the great civilizations on the Pacific littoral and isthmus, whence it gradually leavened the bulk of the vast aboriginal population of the Americas.

[When this communication was made to the Society my sole object was to put together the scattered evidence supplied by the practice of mummification, and other customs associated with it, in substantiation of the fact that the influence of ancient Egyptian civilization, or a particular phase of it, had spread to the Far East and America. Since then so much new information has come to light, not only in confirmation of the main thesis, but also defining the dates of a series of cultural waves, that it will soon be possible, not only to sketch out in some detail the routes taken by the series of ancient mariners who spread abroad this peculiarly distinctive civilization, but also to identify the adventurers and determine the dates of their greatest exploits and the motives for most of their enterprises. In collaboration with Mr. J. W. Perry I hope soon to be ready to attempt that task.

I have deliberately refrained from referring to the vexed question of totemism in this communication, although it is obvious that it is closely connected with the "heliolithic" culture. I have used the expression "serpent worship" in several places where perhaps it would have been more correct to refer to the serpent-totem; but so far from weakening, the consideration of totemism will add to the strength and cogency of my argument.

When I assigned (p. 37) a comparatively late date for the extension of the "heliolithic" culture to the western Mediterranean and beyond I was not aware that Siret (*L'Anthropologie*, T. 20 and 21, 1909-10) had arrived at the same conclusion.]

BIBLIOGRAPHY.[21]

1. D'ALBERTIS, L. M. "New Guinea." London, 1880, Vol. I.

2. ALLEN, F. A. "The Original Range of the Papuan and Negritto Races." *Journ. Anthropol. Inst.*, Vol. 8, 1878-9, p. 38.

3. BANCROFT, H. H. "The Native Races of the Pacific States of North America." London, 1875.

4. BENT, T. "The Bahrein Islands in the Persian Gulf." *Proc. R. Geograph. Soc.*, 1870, p. 13.

5. BLACKMAN, A. M. "The Significance of Incense and Libations in Funerary and Temple Ritual." *Zeitsch. f. Ægypt. Sprache*, Bd. 50.

6. BREASTED, J. H. "A History of Egypt." London, 1906.

7. BROWN, J. MACMILLAN. "Maori and Polynesian." London, 1907.

8. BUCKLAND, A. W. "The Serpent in Connection with Primitive Metallurgy." *Journ. Anthropol. Inst.*, Vol. 4, 1874-5, p. 60.

9. *Ibid.* "Ethnological Hints afforded by the Stimulants in use among Savages and among the Ancients." *Journ. Anthropol. Inst.*, Vol. 8, 1878-9, p. 239.

10. *Ibid.* "On Tattooing." *Journ. Anthropol. Inst.*, Vol. 17, 1887-8, p. 318.

11. CAPART, J. "Une Rue de Tombeaux." *Brussels*, 1907.

12. CROOKE, W. "Northern India." 1907.

13. *Ibid.* "The Rude Stone Monuments of India," *Proc. Cotteswold Naturalists' Field Club*, Vol. XV., May, 1905, p. 117.

14. DAVIDS, T. W. RHYS. "Buddhist India." London, 1911.

15. ELLIS, W. "Polynesian Researches." Vol. I., London, 1832.

16. ENOCH, C. R. "The Secret of the Pacific." London, 1912.

17. FERGUSSON, J. "Rude Stone Monuments in all Countries." London, 1872.

18. FEWKES, J. WALTER. "Great Stone Monuments in History and Geography." Presidential Address delivered before the Anthropological Society of Washington, February 20th, 1912.

19. FLOWER, W. H. "Illustrations of the Mode of preserving the Dead in Darnley Island and in South Australia." *Journ. Anthropol. Inst.*, Vol. 8, 1878-9, p. 389.

---

[21] Many other bibliographical references have been added in the text while this memoir was in course of printing.

20. Fox, A. Lane. "Remarks on Mr. Hodder Westropp's Paper on Cromlechs, with a Map of the World, shewing the Distribution of Megalithic Monuments." *Journ. Ethnol. Soc.*, Vol. 1, 1869, p. 59.

21. *Ibid.* "On Early Modes of Navigation." *Journ. Anthropol. Inst.*, Vol. 4, 1874-5, p. 389.

22. Frazer, John. "The Aborigines of New South Wales." Sydney, 1892.

23. Gardiner, Alan H. Article, "Life and Death." *Hastings' Dictionary of Religion and Ethics*, 1915.

24. Glaumont, M. "Usages, Moeurs, et Coutumes des Néo-Calédoniens." *Revue d'ethnologie*, 1888, p. 73—Summary in Cartailhac's "Materiaux pour l'histoire de l'homme," Vol. 22, 1888, p. 507.

25. Haddon, A. C., and Myers, C. S. "Reports of the Cambridge Anthropological Expedition to Torres Straits." *Funeral Ceremonies*, Vol. VI., Cambridge, 1908, p. 126.

26. Haigh (Miss). "Some Account of the Island of Teneriffe." *Trans. Ethnol Soc.*, New Series, Vol. 7. 1869, p. 112.

27. Hamlyn-Harris, R. "Papuan Mummification." *Memoirs of the Queensland Museum*, Vol. I., 27th Nov., 1912.

28. *Ibid.* "Mummification," *loc. cit. supra.*

29. Harrison, J. Park. "On the Artificial Enlargement of the Earlobe." *Journ. Anthropol. Inst.*, Vol. 2, 1872-3, p. 190.

30. *Ibid.* "Note on Phœnician Characters from Sumatra." *Journ. Anthropol. Inst.*, Vol. 4, 1874, p. 387.

31. Hartman, C. V. "Archæological Researches in Costa Rica." Stockholm, 1901—a Review in *Nature*, March 16th, 1905, p. 462.

32. Hastings' *Dictionary of Religion and Ethics.*

33. Hertz, R. "Contribution à une Étude sur la Représentation Collective de la Mort." *L'Année Sociologique*, 1905-6, p. 48.

34. Hodson, T. C. "Funerary Rites and Eschatological Beliefs of the Assam Hill Tribes." *Third Internat. Congress Hist. Religions*, Oxford, 1908, Vol. 1, p. 58.

35. Hough, W. "Oriental Influences in Mexico." *American Anthropologist*, Vol. 2, 1900, p. 66.

36. *Ibid.* "Culture of the Ancient Pueblos of the Upper Gila River Region, New Mexico and Arizona." *Bulletin 87, Smithsonian Institution*, 1914, p. 132.

37. Hrdlička, A. "Some Results of Recent Anthropological Exploration in Peru." *Smithsonian Miscellaneous Collections*, Vol. 56, No. 16, 1911.

38. Hutchinson, T. J. "Anthropology of Prehistoric Peru." *Journ. Anthropol. Inst.*, Vol. 4, 1874-5, p. 438.

39. JONES, F. WOOD. *In Report on the Archæological Survey of Nubia* for 1907-8, Vol. II., p. 194.

40. JUNKER, H. "Excavations of the Vienna Imperial Academy of Sciences at the Pyramids of Gizah, 1914." *Journ. Egyptian Archæol.*, Vol. I., Oct., 1914, p. 250.

41. KEANE, A. H. "Ethnology." Cambridge, 1896.

42. *Ibid.* "Man, Past and Present." Cambridge, 1900.

43. LORENZ, H. A. "Eenige Maanden onder de Papoea's." 1905, p. 224.

44. LUBBOCK, J. "Notes on the Macas Indians." *Journ. Anthropol. Inst.*, Vol. 3, 1873-4, p. 29.

45. MACE, A. C. "The Early Dynastic Cemeteries of Naga-ed-Dêr, Part II." 1909.

46. MOLL, HERMANN. "Modern History." Vol. I., Dublin, 1739.

47. MYERS, C. S. "Contributions to Egyptian Anthropology: Tatuing." *Journ. Anthropol. Inst.*, Vol. XXXIII., 1903, p. 82.

48. NADAILLAC DE. "L'Amérique Préhistorique." Paris, 1883.

49. NUTTALL, ZELIA. "The Fundamental Principles of Old and New World Civilizations," Archæological and Ethnological Papers of the Peabody Museum, Cambridge, Mass., 1901, p. 602.

50. *Ibid.* "A curious Survival in Mexico of the Purpura Shell-Fish for Dyeing." Putnam Anniversary Volume, 1909.

51. OLDHAM, C. F. "The Sun and the Serpent." London, 1905.

52. PAGE, H. "Post-mortem artificially-contracted Indian Heads." *Journ. Anat. and Phys.*, Vol. 31, 1897, p. 252.

53. PARTINGTON, EDGE. "Ethnographical Album of the Pacific Islands." 3rd series, August, 1898, p. 94.

54. PETRIE, W. M. FLINDERS. "Tarkhan." 1913 and 1914.

55. PERROT and CHIPIEZ. "History of Art in Phœnicia." London, 1885.

56. PETTIGREW, T. J. "A History of Egyptian Mummies." London, 1834.

57. PIORRY. Article "Massage," in *Dictionnaire des Sciences Médicales*. 1819.

58. PRESCOTT, W. H. "Conquest of Peru."

59. *Ibid.* "Conquest of Mexico."

60. QUATREFAGES, A. DE. "Hommes Fossiles et Hommes Sauvages." Paris, 1884.

61. READ, C. H., JOYCE, T. A., and EDGE-PARTINGTON, J. "Handbook of the Ethnological Collections" (British Museum), 1910.

62. REISNER, GEORGE A. *Bulletin of the Boston Museum of Fine Arts.* Vol. XII., No. 69, April, 1914, p. 23.

63. REUTTER, L. "De l'embaumement avant et après Jésus-Christ." Paris, 1912.

64. RIVERS, W. H. R. Presidential Address to Section H. *Report Brit. Assoc.*, Portsmouth, 1911, p. 490, or *Nature*, 1911, Vol. LXXXVII., p. 356.

65. *Ibid.* "The Disappearance of Useful Arts." *Report Brit. Assoc.*, 1912, p. 598 [Abstract of a memoir published in *Festsscrift Tillägnad Edvard Wester-marck*, Helsingfors, 1912, p. 109].

66. *Ibid.* "Survival in Sociology." *The Sociological Review*, October, 1913, p. 292.

67. *Ibid.* "Massage in Melanesia." *Report of the 17th International Congress of Medicine*, London, August, 1913, Section XXIII., History of Medicine.

68. *Ibid.* "The Contact of Peoples." Essays and Studies presented to William Ridgeway. Cambridge, p. 474.

69. *Ibid.* "The History of Melanesian Society." Cambridge, 1914, Vol. II.

70. *Ibid.* "Is Australian Culture Simple or Complex?" *Report Brit. Assoc.*, 1914; also *Man*, 1914, p. 172.

71. ROTH, W. E. "North Queensland Ethnography, Bulletin No. 9, Burial Ceremonies and Disposal of the Dead." *Records of the Australian Museum*, Sydney, Vol. VI., No. 5, 1907, p. 365.

72. ROSCOE, J. "Further Notes on the Manners and Customs of the Baganda." *Journal of the Anthropological Institute*, Vol. XXXII., 1902, p. 44. [Also his book entitled "The Baganda."]

73. SEMPLE, ELLEN C. "Influences of Geographic Environment on the basis of Ratzel's System of Anthropo-Geography." London, 1911.

74. SETHE, KURT. "Zur altaegyptischen Sage vom Sonnenauge das in der Fremde war." *Untersuchungen zur Gesch. u. Altertumskunde Aeg.*, Bd. V., Heft 3, 1912, p. 10.

75. SMITH, G. ELLIOT. "On the Natural Preservation of the Brain in the Ancient Egyptians." *Journal of Anatomy and Physiology*, Vol. XXXVI., pp. 375-380. Two text figures. 1902.

76. *Ibid.* "The physical characters of the mummy of the Pharaoh Thothmosis IV." *Annales du Service des Antiquités de l'Égypte*, 1904, [and in Carter and Newberry's "Tomb of Thothmosis IV." London, 1908].

77. *Ibid.* "Report on four mummies of the XXI. dynasty." Ibid., 1904.

78. *Ibid.* "A Contribution to the Study of Mummification in Egypt." *Mémoires presentés à l'Institut Égyptien*, Tome V., Fascicule I., 1906, pp. 1-54, 19 plates.

79. *Ibid.* "An Account of the Mummy of a Priestess of Amen." *Annales du Service des Antiquités de l'Égypte*, 1906, pp. 1-28, 9 plates.

80. *Ibid.* "Report on the Unrolling of the Mummies of the Kings Siptah, Seti II., Ramses IV., Ramses V., and Ramses VI., in the Cairo Museum." *Bulletin de l'Institut Égyptien*, 5ᵉ Série, T.I. pp. 45 à 67.

81. *Ibid.* "Report on the Unwrapping of the Mummy of Menephtah." *Annales du Service des Antiquités*, 1907.

82. *Ibid.* "Notes on Mummies." *The Cairo Scientific Journal*, February, 1908.

83. *Ibid.* "On the Mummies in the Tomb of Amenhotep II." *Bulletin de l'Institut Égyptien*, 5ᵉ Série, Tome I., 1908.

84. *Ibid.* Account of the Mummies of Yuaa and Thuiu, in Quibell's "Tomb of Yuaa and Thuiu." Catalogue Général du Musée du Caïre, 1908.

85. *Ibid.* "The History of Mummification in Egypt." *Proc. Royal Philosophical Society of Glasgow*, 1910.

86. *Ibid.* "The Royal Mummies." Catalogue Général des Antiquités Égyptiennes du Musée du Caïre, 1912.

87. *Ibid.* "Egyptian Mummies." *Journal of Egyptian Archæology*, Vol. I., Part III., July, 1914, p. 189.

88. *Ibid.* "Heart and Reins." *Journal of the Manchester Oriental Society*, Vol. I., 1911, p. 41.

89. *Ibid.* "The Earliest Evidence of Attempts at Mummification in Egypt." *Report Brit. Assoc.*, 1912, p. 612.

90. *Ibid.* "The Ancient Egyptians." London and New York, 1911.

91. *Ibid.* "The Influence of Egypt under the Ancient Empire." *Report Brit. Assoc.*, 1911; also Man, 1911, p. 176.

92. *Ibid.* "Megalithic Monuments and their Builders." *Report Brit. Assoc.*, 1912, p. 607; also *Man*, 1912, p. 173.

93. *Ibid.* "The Origin of the Dolmen." *Report Brit. Assoc.*, 1913; also *Man*, 1913, p. 193.

94. *Ibid.* "The Evolution of the Rock-cut Tomb and the Dolmen." Essays and Studies presented to William Ridgeway. Cambridge, 1913, p. 493.

95. *Ibid.* "Report on the Physical Characters of the Ancient Egyptians." *Report Brit. Assoc.*, 1914; also *Man*, 1914, p. 172.

96. *Ibid.* "Early Racial Migrations and the Spread of Certain Customs." *Report Brit. Assoc.*, 1914; also *Man*, 1914, p. 173.

97. *Ibid.* "The Rite of Circumcision." *Journ. Manchester Egy. and Oriental Soc.*, 1913, p. 75.

98. SMITH, PERCY. "Hawaiki." London, 3rd Edn., 1910.

99. TALBOT, P. AMAURY. "Some Ibibio Customs and Beliefs." *Journ. African Soc.*, 1914, p. 241.

100. TAYLOR, MEADOWS. "On Prehistoric Archæology of India." *Journ. Ethnol. Soc.*, New Series, Vol. I., 1868-9, p. 157.

101. THURSTON, E. "The Madras Presidency," 1913.

102. TYLOR, E. B. "On the Diffusion of Mythical Beliefs as Evidence in the History of Culture." *Report Brit. Assoc.*, 1894, p. 774.

103. WAKE, C. S. "Origin of Serpent Worship." *Journ. Anthropol. Inst.*, Vol. 2, 1872-3.

104. Weeks, J. H. "Anthropological Notes on the Bangala of the Upper Congo River." *Journ. Roy. Anthropol. Inst.*, Vol. XXXIX., 1909, pp. 450 and 451.

105. Wilson, Thomas. "The Swastika." *Report of Smithsonian Institution*, 1896.

106. Yarrow, H. C. "A further Contribution to the Study of the North American Indians." *1st Report, Bureau Amer. Ethnol.*, Washington, 1881.

LECTOR HOUSE LLP
E-MAIL: lectorpublishing@gmail.com